KNITTING VINTAGE SOCKS

New Twists on Classic Patterns

Nancy Bush

INTERWEAVE.
interweavebooks.com

D1295754

Illustrator: Gayle Ford
Photo Stylist: Ann Swanson
Designer: Bren Frisch
Back cover photo: Joe Gardner

©, 2005 Nancy Bush
Photography (except as noted) © 2005, Interweave Press LLC
Images from *Weldon's Practical Needlework*: pp. 2, 3, 17, 19, 21, 22, 23, 34, 39, 43, 47, 50, 54, 59, 62, 66, 70, 75, 79, 87, 90, 94, 98, 102, 107, 111.

Interweave Press LLC
201 East Fourth Street
Loveland, CO 80537 USA
interweavebooks.com

Printed in China through Asia Pacific Offset

Library of Congress Cataloging-in-Publication Data

Bush, Nancy, 1951-
  Knitting vintage socks : new twists on classic patterns / Nancy Bush.
      p. cm.
  Includes bibliographical references and index.
  ISBN 978-1-931499-65-1
  1. Knitting—Patterns. 2. Socks. I. Title.
  TT825.B894 2005
  746.43'20432--dc22
                                                2005003010

10 9 8 7 6 5

ACKNOWLEDGMENTS

My interest in knitting socks began many years ago and was encouraged by Elaine Rowley at *Knitter's Magazine*. Elaine published my first sock patterns and gave me the opportunity to begin thinking about feet in a whole new way.

This book seemed a natural progression after *Folk Socks* and *Knitting on the Road* (Interweave Press, 1994 and 2001). Looking back at history has always been one of my greatest pleasures, and thinking about nineteenth-century knitters while I worked on this book has been intriguing. I wish to thank Marilyn Murphy and Linda Ligon at Interweave Press for agreeing that the idea for the book was a good one and for their enthusiasm for the project, also Jeane Hutchins, who encouraged me to take a closer look, answered many questions, and gave me advice about this period of history.

I had a lot of help, advice, and encouragement at Interweave Press from Betsy Armstrong who welcomed me as I pursued my quest. I was thrilled to be able to go through all the original volumes of *Weldon's* and to discover the many interesting sock patterns they contained.

After deciding which patterns I wanted to use, I spent many hours deciphering a sea of small gray type while I translated the patterns from nineteenth-century English to today's knitting language. Then came the knitting. I had a wonderful group of skilled knitters to help me—knitting sock mates and checking patterns to make sure I didn't leave anything out. With heartfelt appreciation, I wish to thank Betsy Campbell, Jill Dahle, Margaret Hevel, Karen Hevel-Mingo, Brith Otterud, Margene Smith, Fritzy White, and Marge Yee-Norrander for all their help and advice.

iv

"After finally deciding which patterns I wanted to use,

Many thanks to my friends Patrick de Freitas, who gave much needed advice and explanations about English language and history, Vonnie Wildfoerster, who was available at all times to help me make decisions and listen to my musings, and Marsha Thomas for her wise advice.

I had many questions about yarns from the past. From Britain, Rowena Edlin-White sent me the Walker Bell Gauge and much appreciated information on yarns and needle sizes. I also had help from members of the Knitting and Crochet Guild in the United Kingdom, including Rita Taylor and Lesley O'Connell, who offered thoughts and information on yarns of bygone times.

This book would not be nearly so wonderful or beautiful without the experts at Interweave Press. Editor Ann Budd's good sense and humor made every part of the process a treat. She took great care with every detail and knitted a few of the mates as well. Technical editing is something that I am in awe of, and Lori Gayle did a fantastic job of that. Many thanks to Bren Frisch, who created the cover and interior design, to Ann Swanson for photostyling, to Gayle Ford for illustrations, and especially to Joe Coca for his (always) exceptional photographs.

I appreciate the attention to detail by Dean Howes for the production work, Stephen Beal for copy editing, and Nancy Arndt for proofreading and indexing.

I had constant attention while I worked on this book from Mac, the newest canine member of our household, and was lovingly reminded many times to "go knit" or to "come for a walk" by my sweetheart, Joe. Yet again, Joe, I couldn't have done it without you!

v

I spent many hours deciphering a sea of small gray type."

Contents

INTRODUCTION

When I first began thinking about the task of taking sock patterns from the *Weldon's Practical Needlework* series and putting them into a modern context, I was excited by the chance to scrutinize knitting from nineteenth-century Britain and curious to see what I would uncover in the process.

After I got used to the small print and almost chatty ways the patterns were written, what I found was a collection of very interesting designs that paid much attention to detail. I discovered patterns that were logical in their design, and pieces that were fun to knit.

One obstacle: Yarns were described in the text as "pretty" or "soft," but there was no information on yardage, on the weight of specific balls or skeins, or, most importantly, on gauge. As a modern knitter, I felt lost without that information, but I simply decided to go with what I thought would work with the yarns available to me today—along with my common sense—and give the patterns a try.

Another obstacle loomed, however: Many of the patterns called for the equivalent of size 000 or 0000 (1.5 or 1.25 mm) needles. Yes, these sizes are still available, but I felt that few knitters today would enjoy knitting with such small needles. As I went through the patterns, I determined whether the sock would work well on larger needles than called for and with the yarns I had chosen by noting the number of stitches to cast on and the number of stitches in the heel and foot.

"I found a collection of interesting designs that paid much attention to detail."

Beyond such technicalities, I enjoyed thinking about the times when the patterns were written and wondered about the person or persons who actually designed and wrote them. *Weldon's* never mentions these people—they are anonymous. And it's important to remember that the patterns were written at a time when

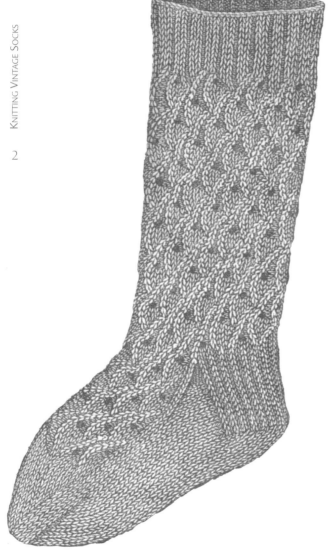

pattern writing and printing for the masses was a fairly new concept. Knitting techniques had been around a long while, but setting the process down on paper was something new. Our ways of writing patterns have evolved—for example, where words were spelled out in the past, they are abbreviated today.

The text that accompanied the patterns told what a specific piece was designed for, be it hunting or cycling, keeping a cab driver warm on a cold winter's night, or delighting a girl of twelve with a pair of pretty socks. Many of the issues also contained advertisements for other *Weldon's* publications such as novels and useful instruction for young wives or hints on etiquette. There was often a section titled "What our Readers Think of Us." These sections contain testimonials describing how happy readers were with the magazine in general, or how nicely projects turned out and how pleased the reader was with the results. I imagined one of the sisters in E. M. Forster's novel *Howard's End* sitting down and writing to *Weldon's* to say that the stockings she just finished were perfect and she couldn't wait for her next issue to arrive.

While fashions have changed dramatically since these magazines were published, it is interesting to see that socks haven't changed that much. We use almost the same construction techniques today that knitters used a hundred or more years ago. And while our yarns may be spun from blends of stronger, longer-wearing fibers, and are more colorful than what was common in the past, the end product is not much different now from what it was then.

"Beyond technicalities, I enjoyed thinking about the times when the

The *Weldon's Practical Needlework* magazines were bound into a series of book volumes. They are not only a collection of patterns, they are a window into the past that displays all the fussy articles of clothing that were then the height of fashion, along with the household decorations that made a living space comfortable and attractive. I enjoyed looking into that window by searching for small bits of trivial history—such as when the tea bag was invented (1904)—and trying to put these publications into their own place in time even as I transported their patterns into the twenty-first century.

I hope that as you read and knit from this book you will be able to look through that window to see your own picture of the past, one which produced many of the ways we do our knitting today, as well as so many other parts of our life.

3

patterns were written and wondered about the persons who designed them."

A BRIEF HISTORY OF WELDON'S PRACTICAL NEEDLEWORK

Weldon's Practical Needlework began monthly publication in 1886 and continued until the end of the 1920s. They were the inspiration of Mrs. Weldon (no first name was ever given), who began *The Ladies Journal* in 1879, an endeavor that encouraged many other publications in the needlework field. Each *Practical Needlework* issue, printed in leaflet form, contained fourteen pages and was devoted to specific forms of needlework including crochet, tatting, smocking, macramé, netting, crewel, various types of embroidery, and knitting. Each technique was presented in a series of leaflets. The series for each technique were published in chronological order, but there could be lapses of months (or years) between two sequential series. Stocking knitting had its own category, with many issues devoted just to socks and stockings. The issues were undated until 1915, after which they were dated with the month and year. There is never any mention of an editorial staff or designers.

The price for a monthly issue in 1886 was 2 pence—a penny was one-twelfth of an old English shilling, about .01 of a U.S. dollar—and the price was not raised until 1916 when it went up to 3d (3 pence). The publishers kept all back issues in print to provide knitters and needleworkers in the late 1800s and early twentieth century with a wealth of information. Starting around 1888, each year's issues were bound into a separate volume that cost 2 shillings and 6 pence.

By the time the *Weldon's* publications began, handknitting in Britain was a well-established craft. Richard Rutt, in *A*

History of Hand Knitting (Interweave Press, 2003), writes that caps seem to have been the first knitted items known in Britain: Caps found in Coventry are dated from the thirteenth century. Professional knitters were organized as early as 1424, and it may have been they who made the Coventry caps.

EARLY HANDKNITTED STOCKINGS

Handknitted stockings first appear in British knitting history during the reign of Henry VIII (1509–1547). A stocking leg or possibly a knitted sleeve, along with knitted caps and other knitted fragments, were recovered from the Mary Rose, Henry's flagship, which sank in 1545. These pieces were found on the decks inhabited by seamen or soldiers, not the areas where officers lived or worked, so the supposition is that knitting was becoming part of everyday life at that time. This theory remains unproven because it is not known if the knitting was done in England or if the articles of clothing happened to be castoffs from more wealthy persons aboard the ship.

By the time of Edward VI's reign (1547–1553), the knitting of stockings is clearly documented. Records from 1550, a time when woolen knitwear was being made for children and the working class, show that 12 pence was paid for a pair of knit hose for a little boy named Francis Willoughby. By 1572, the craft of knitting was known throughout England, and knitted stockings had become the norm.

Royal records from subsequent reigns attest to the making and use of knitted stockings in Britain. During her short reign, Mary I (1553–1558) was given four pairs of hose "of garnsey making" by Sir

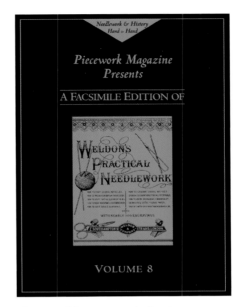

The original fourteen-page leaflets have been published in facsimile editions by Interweave Press.

Leonard Chamberlain, and Mary, Queen of Scots wore handknitted stockings when she was executed in 1587.

It was during Queen Elizabeth's long reign (1558–1603) that the technique of knitting became thoroughly established throughout Britain. The story of the Queen's delight with the handknitted black silk stockings she received as a gift in 1560 from her silk woman, Mistress Montague, is well documented. Afterward, the Queen abandoned her cloth stockings forever and wore only silk stockings "because they are so pleasant, fine and delicate" (Richard Rutt, *A History of Handknitting*).

Whether this story about Elizabeth is true or not, such silk stockings could only have been knitted once the manufacture of fine-gauge metal knitting needles had

Source: Dover

been perfected. Making metal needles from steel rods required a very high level of expertise. The craft of drawing steel through plates with holes made thin needles generally available, which led to the expansion of fine-gauge handknitting. It seems that the skill of making fine needles was known in Italy and Spain earlier than elsewhere, and it may have been in one of these two countries that Elizabeth's fine silk stockings actually originated.

Once handknitted stockings became a part of both high fashion and everyday life in Britain, knitting schools were created to teach this useful skill to poor children to "keep them from mischief and relieve their poverty," according to Rutt. The oldest knitting pattern for socks was published in *Natura Extenterata* or *Nature Unbowelled*, a medical compendium published in 1655. We can be grateful that Rutt translates this pattern in his book because the original was written in one very long sentence and toe shaping was not included.

A MEANS OF LIVELIHOOD

By the mid-seventeenth century, people throughout the British countryside were knitting for their livelihood and continued to do so for the next two centuries. To give an idea of how pervasive knitting was in the United Kingdom, it was reported in 1799 that in one single parish 10,000 people were employed knitting stockings. Through the nineteenth century, many thousands of pairs of British stockings were shipped to Europe and North America.

Beginning with the wool itself, the manufacture of woolen goods helped Britain become a powerful leader in politics and trade worldwide. There is a reason why the Lord Chancellor, Speaker of the House of Lords, sits on a seat stuffed with wool—a woolsack—when meetings are in session. Initiated during King Edward III's reign (1327–1377), the woolsack was originally stuffed with English wool to honor the wool trade, England's traditional source of wealth. Today, it is stuffed with wool from each of the countries in the British Commonwealth as a sign of unity.

It was this great interest in and need for manufactured woolen goods, be they woven or knitted, that created the environment for the Industrial Revolution. One very early foreshadowing of this important development was the invention of the knitting frame by William Lee in the late 1500s. It was received with little enthusiasm in England because it was regarded as a threat to the livelihood of handknitters. In any case, Lee's frame was the first attempt to mechanize textile work; as the industry continued to grow in the eighteenth and early nineteenth centuries, thought turned more and more toward making textile work faster and less costly.

THE INDUSTRIAL REVOLUTION

The Industrial Revolution began about 1750 and continued for a hundred years. In Britain, changes in the way manufacturing was done created a shift from a rural to urban economy. Steam power and coal replaced muscle power, and many jobs that were done by hand at home were moved into factories where they were done by machines like the spinning jenny and power loom; knitting machines soon followed.

As new products appeared, new roads and waterways, the railroad, and telegraph communication increased manufacturers' ability to sell and move goods. The distribution of wealth increased when iron and steel construction was improved and factory labor was developed. Large cities grew from small towns, and political and social change was rapid. Instruction in

household management and the necessary skills in sewing or related activities had earlier been handed down from mother to daughter; schools were now set up to teach these skills as a means of livelihood for the poorer classes. It was not until the end of the Napoleonic Wars in 1815 that what we think of as leisure knitting began to emerge. International trade allowed such items as merino wool to be imported. Home knitting and needlepoint were furthered by the availability of "Berlin" wool, a German-made yarn in luscious colors.

London's Victoria and Albert Museum contains examples from this time of "drawing room" knitting, small items such as pincushions and purses. Quite different from the rough stockings knitted by country folk, these were luxurious items decorated with beads or pretty patterns. They were likely made by upper-class ladies for entertainment, as gifts, or perhaps if the women's circumstances were reduced, for sale. Queen Victoria's husband, Prince Albert of Saxe-Coburg-Gotha, enjoyed reading to the Queen while she knitted.

By the 1830s, knitting became fashionable among the educated classes. The first English knitting books were published

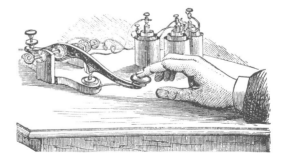

Telegraph communication increased manufacturers' ability to sell and move goods. Source: Dover

in 1835 and 1840, followed by a number of published patterns and "knitting recipe" books. The first mass-market woman's magazine, the *Englishwoman's Domestic Magazine,* was published in 1852 by Samuel Orchart Beeton. This publication became popular in part for the pieces on domestic management written by Beeton's wife Isabella.

Victoria's example of high morality during her long reign (1837–1901) greatly influenced life in Britain. There was relative prosperity and the family was regarded as the central institution. Duty, earnestness, and hard work; these were the moral attributes of the time. Thrift was of utmost importance, and comportment and personal behavior were scrutinized. Changes taking place in thought, attitude, and ability were rapid. In 1852, English philosopher Herbert Spencer coined the term "evolution," and in 1859, Darwin wrote *The Origin of Species.*

So many things were happening to make life easier—both the self-adhesive envelope and the snap fastener were invented in 1860. Patented in 1863, linoleum helped change the way floors were covered and cleaned.

Women were beginning to think more "liberal" thoughts at this time and they were taking on new challenges. Elizabeth

Women were beginning to think more "liberal" thoughts. Source: Dover

Garnett Anderson (1836–1917) was the first woman to qualify in medicine in Britain, and she pioneered professional education for women. She was the first woman doctor in Britain, the first female member of the British Medical Association, the first female dean of a medical school, and the first woman mayor in British history. A tribute written by her daughter after her death at eighty-one states that "She helped to tear down one after another the barriers which, since the beginning of history, hindered woman from work and progress and light and service." On a lighter note, in 1853 woman's rights campaigner Amelia Jenks Bloomer loaned her name to the "bloomers" that gave women much more freedom of movement.

Influenced by artists such as William Morris (1834–1896), a prolific writer, craftsman, painter, and social reformer, the Arts and Crafts movement began in Britain in the 1880s. The ideals of the movement were founded on a rejection of the fussiness of Victorian design and anger toward some of the results of industrialization, along with a rebirth of interest in handmade craft and art.

Weldon's Practical Needlework was born into this climate, at a time in history when doing handwork was becoming a pleasure for leisure, rather than a livelihood or chore indicative of a frugal life; thus *Weldon's* attracted a new, more educated class of women with some income. That said, knitting on Sundays was still forbidden in some English households up to the 1930s.

The early issues of all the *Weldon's Practical Needlework* series, including the *Practical Knitter* and *Practical Stocking*

Knitter, are illustrated with reproductions of drawings of the items offered. Later issues attest to advancements in print media with patterns illustrated by photographs of items or models wearing the garments.

The fashions of the times are well represented in the pages of *Weldon's*. Hairstyles and clothing for newly popular hobbies like golf and bicycling are evident. One issue of the *Practical Knitter* is devoted to dolls and doll clothing, and another offers instruction for knitting initials, figures, and "clox" (clocks) in stockings.

IN RETROSPECT

From a distance of eighty years, it's hard to tell exactly why *Weldon's* stopped publication in the 1920s. Perhaps the main editors retired; perhaps the publisher decided to move on to more profitable opportunities. More likely, fashion changed and the 1920s were not suited to magazines like *Weldon's*.

Here we are at the dawn of a new century, and times have changed again. We are in the midst of a renewed enthusiasm for handknitting. The patterns found in *Weldon's* can be regarded with new insight and fresh ideas. While some antique patterns are impractical for today's lifestyles, others remain as timely

Influenced by artist William Morris, the Arts and Crafts movement began in Britain in the 1880s. Photo courtesy of the Board of Trustees of the Victoria and Albert Museum, Bridgeman Art Library, London/SuperStock.

as they were when they were designed. Perhaps a design can be used today for a different purpose, age of wearer, or even gender, but the interest and excitement found in the patterns endures. Interweave Press's republication of the *Weldon's* volumes enables us to learn from the best of the past.

UPDATING *WELDON'S* TECHNIQUES

The first issue of the first series of *Weldon's Practical Stocking Knitter*, found in Volume 1 of *Weldon's Practical Needlework*, was published in 1886. The subtitle is "How to Knit every kind of Stocking for Ladies, Gentlemen and Children."

The text states that handknitted stockings are more durable and economical than woven (i.e., machine-knitted) ones, are easier to repair, and, if they are made well and washed carefully, can be refooted at least three times. It encourages stocking knitting as "pleasant work for winter evenings, not trying to the eyes, and not any hindrance to conversation." Knitting stockings is also "convenient for taking up at odd moments" and progresses quickly. Let us note that *Weldon's* stockings were often knitted on U.S. size 000 (1.5 mm) or 0000 (1.25 mm) needles, so quick progress is relative. *Weldon's* philosophy was that every lady should be "au fait" (skilled) with the art of stocking knitting.

This early series discusses materials and general instructions for knitting stockings: casting on, working in a round, and shaping the leg. There are instructions and illustrations for nine ways to shape heels, ways to reheel stockings and socks, and seven ways to shape toes.

Volume 20, Sixty-first Series, published in 1905, offers an updated discussion of materials and a definition of knitting terms. The latter has proved most helpful for "translating" *Weldon's* patterns into our modern knitting language.

Materials discussed in both these series are described as "soft," "smooth," "durable," in a "medium" or "fine" size, "pleasant to use and satisfactory in wear." The weight or yardage of individual skeins or balls is not mentioned, and never, in any pattern I have studied in *Weldon's*, is there ever any mention of gauge.

We are told that knitting needles are available in steel, ivory, wood, imitation amber, tortoiseshell, and vulcanite. Steel needles are deemed best for stocking work and they came in 6½" (16.5 cm) or 9" (23 cm) lengths. They should have "nicely tapered points" at both ends. *Weldon's* standard for sizing needles is a Walker's Bell Gauge. Needles were measured by fitting into the slot on the sides, not the holes, as on gauges available today.

A Walker's Bell Gauge was used to measure standard needle sizes.

NEEDLE EQUIVALENTS		
British	U.S.	Metric
18	000000	0.75 mm
17	00000	1 mm
16	0000	1.25 mm
15	000	1.5 mm
14	00	1.75 mm
	0	2 mm
13	1	2.25 mm
12	2	2.75 mm
11		3 mm
10	3	3.25 mm

GENERAL RULES FOR STOCKING KNITTING

Below are selected instructions from the first *Weldon's Practical Stocking Knitter*, Volume 1, First Series and *Weldon's Practical Knitter*, Volume 20, Sixty-first Series. The instructions quoted from *Weldon's* are in shown in yellow boxes. I've added my comments after the quotes.

QUALITY OF KNITTING

> Try and knit with regularity, neither too loose nor too tight; if too loose the work will draw out of shape in the washing, and if too tight the wool gets impoverished. The happy medium is when the stitches will slip just easily along the needle.

> Knitting should be neither too tight nor too loose; the stitches should slip just easily along the needles, and yet not be so loose as to permit any falling off unawares; if too loose the stitches will set unevenly and the work will be untidy, and on the other hand tight knitting will cause the wool to thin and spoil for the want of needful "spring."

These quotes from *Weldon's*, one from Volume 1 and the other from Volume 20, impress upon the knitter how important it is to keep a "happy medium" when knitting, and to take care in making each stitch.

CAST-ONS

> Cast on and off rather loosely and at the casting on, leave the tag end of wool to show where the round begins.

The cast-on offered in the basic knitting text in *Weldon's*, Volume 1, First Series, is a "knitting on" cast-on (Glossary, page 113). For socks, I prefer the Continental (also known as long-tail) cast-on (Glossary, page 113) and have used it for all my interpretations.

Many of the sock designs in *Weldon's* call for casting on with the yarn doubled. Doubled yarn gives a more elastic cast-on than single yarn. To do a double cast-on, take two ends of yarn, either from two separate balls of yarn or one end from the outside and one from the inside of a single ball, and cast on holding both yarns together. When you've cast on the desired number of stitches, break off one end of yarn, leaving a tail for weaving in later, and continue knitting as usual with the other end.

When you're casting on with a single yarn, it's a good idea to cast on over two needles held parallel, removing one of them (carefully) when you finish the cast-on. Using two needles to cast on will give you an elastic edge and facilitate working the first round.

11

JOINS

I couldn't find a single description in *Weldon's* of how to join stitches into a round, and that's surprising considering that a hole or loose stitch can occur if a join isn't carefully worked. Turn to the Glossary (page 115) for three types of joins that I routinely use; all are easy to work and all form a nearly invisible connection.

WORKING IN ROUNDS

Rounds are knitted in a circle with four or more needles; rows are worked forwards and backwards on two needles only. When knitting in rows, be careful to slip the first stitch in every row, whether doing plain or purl, so as to produce a smooth edge; and when working in rounds keep the first two and the last two stitches of each needle rather tighter than the rest, to prevent the appearance of a gap.

Although the *Weldon's* text discusses using four or more needles, and even illustrates the use of four needles to carry the stitches in the first *Practical Stocking Knitter*, all the patterns I have reviewed call for carrying the stitches on three needles and knitting with a fourth—the classic British method of working circularly with double-pointed needles. Until recent years, British manufacturers packaged needles in sets of only four, while other manufacturers (German, for instance) packaged needles in sets of five. Whether to use four or five needles is a matter of personal taste; either way is acceptable. If the pattern on the instep is complicated, you may want to place all of the instep stitches onto one needle for ease of working the pattern. There are times, however, when it makes sense to use five needles. For example, if the stitch pattern is easily divided into fourths, you may find it easier to keep track of the pattern by carrying the stitches on four needles and knitting with the fifth. Likewise, if there are a large number of stitches, they will be less crowded if carried on four needles instead of three. Carrying your stitches on four needles also puts less strain where the needles meet, and doing so can help to eliminate the ladder effect that sometimes occurs at these places. Most of the instructions in this book are written for working with four needles: three to carry the stitches and a fourth to knit with. But feel free to add a fifth needle if you want— simply divide the instep stitches between two needles instead of carrying them all on a single needle.

Many knitters tend to work purl stitches a bit looser than knit stitches, a tendency that can be compounded at the boundaries between needles. For this reason, it's a good idea to arrange the stitches so that each needle begins with a knit stitch. For example, set up the stitches for ribbing so that each needle begins with a knit stitch and ends with a purl stitch. Doing so may require redistributing the stitches during areas of patterning on the leg or foot, then rearranging the stitches to specified needles before beginning the heel or toe. If you decide to adjust the stitches on the needles, remember to mark the first stitch of the round.

SEAM STITCH

The seam-stitch must begin either with the very first round of the stocking, or with the first round next after the ribbing is completed; it must be marked and particular attention paid to keeping it in a straight line, as upon it the whole shaping of the stocking depends. The seam-stitch may either be purled in every round or purled in one round and knitted in the next.

The decreasings occur on each side of the seam-stitch, at intervals varying from six to ten rounds. They occupy a length from four to six inches, and reduce the stitches to three-fourths the number originally cast on.

You'll find a good example of shaping worked around a seam stitch in the Cycling or Golf Stockings on page 48. These socks begin with 80 stitches at the upper leg and taper (through decreases) to 60 stitches at the ankle.

CHANGING COLORS

When changing the color in ribbing, the right side of the knitting should be next to you (this is for knitting in rows) and the first row or round of the new color must be knitted plain (not ribbed).

Knitting the first round of a new color creates a clean line at the boundary between the two colors. If you rib the first round of a new color, the "purl bump" part of the stitch will be in the old color, and the boundary between the two rounds will be less distinct.

When knitting a stocking in stripes round and round always change the color at the seam-stitch, and knit the seam-stitch with both wools together, so making an almost invisible join; do not break off the wool, but carry it (on the wrong side) from stripe to stripe; whatever ends of wool you are obliged to leave, darn in with a rug needle when the stocking is finished.

This is good advice.

If knitting a stocking in stripes longitudinally down the leg, instead of round and round, it is necessary to knit the wool in, not leave it in long loops. To accomplish this, before knitting a stitch put the wool not in use over the wool you are knitting with, on the wrong side close under the needle, both wools are thus twisted together in the knitting of every stitch. Stockings knitted in this manner are doubly thick and warm.

When knitting stripes or colored patterns down the leg, you must avoid long floats of the unused yarn along the wrong side of the work. Do this by placing the yarn not in use over the yarn that's being knitted (on the wrong side of the work), twisting the two yarns around each other, and thereby securing the carried yarn.

INCREASES AND DECREASES

> Count the stitches after increasing or decreasing to be sure of retaining the right number.

Throughout this book I have used the "make 1" method (Glossary, page 115) of increasing. For the left-leaning decreases, I have followed *Weldon's* practice of using the "sl 1, k1, psso" method (Glossary, page 114). This decrease has the same effect as today's popular "ssk" decrease (Glossary, page 114), but there is no evidence that "ssk" was in general use when *Weldon's* materials were written. However, feel free to make this substitution if you'd like—the results will be the same.

JOINING NEW YARN

> To unite two wools together—When a ball of wool gets used up it is, of course, needful to take another ball to continue the knitting. The two ends of wool should be very carefully united. A common knot is untrustworthy, and unless skillfully managed is unsightly; some very good knitters employ a "weaver's knot." But the really best plan is to lap the ends of wools reversely side by side for about two inches and knit a few stitches with both wools at the same time; this makes a neat and smooth join, and when in the next row you knit the double thickness of the wools the join is almost imperceptible, and is firm and secure.

Never put knots in your knitting—they are likely to come undone! If you're working with pure wool or wool blended with another animal fiber (such as mohair), use the splice method (Glossary, page 115) to join a new ball of yarn. Otherwise, overlap the ends of the old and new balls of yarn and work one stitch with both yarns, then drop the old and continue knitting with the new. When you've finished knitting, thread the ends on a tapestry needle and work them into the wrong side of the sock.

HEEL FLAP

> When the ankle is sufficiently long, place half the stitches, with the seam-stitch in the middle, on one needle for the heel, and divide the other half of the stitches equally on two needles for the instep, these will not be wanted until the heel is finished.

Many of the patterns I have chosen for the pattern section call for a seam stitch running down the leg, and even down the heel flap and through the heel turn. This seam stitch, which provides a focal point for turning the heel, can be very useful for keeping track of your stitches while you're turning the heel. If you don't want a purled seam stitch in the heel, substitute a knit stitch and mark it so you can identify it as the center stitch. You can also eliminate the seam stitch from the heel turn altogether, but if you do, be sure to adjust the stitch count accordingly.

> The heel, when finished and laid down flat, should be just as long as the ankle is wide.

A classic way to work a heel flap is to knit as many rows as there are stitches in the flap, usually half the number of stitches at the ankle.

GUSSETS

Pick up along the flap of the heel as many stitches as with any there may be left on the pin at the top of the heel and those on the instep will restore for the gusset knitting about eight or ten stitches less than the number cast on for the stocking. These "picked-up" stitches should come in rightly to produce the required number, but if the loops along the flap are not sufficiently numerous, increase one stitch in every five, or one stitch in every six, to remedy the deficiency.

This rather convoluted instruction refers to long stockings that begin high up the leg with a lot of stitches. Today, it is common to pick up half as many stitches along the edges of the heel flap as you have rows in the heel flap. For example, if you have 32 stitches in your heel flap, work 32 rows. By slipping (purlwise) the first stitch of every row, you will end up with 16 chain stitches on each edge of the flap. Pick up into these 16 chain stitches. If you need to pick up more stitches along the heel flap edge than there are chains to pick up into, pick up the entire chain loop (both sides) on your needle and knit into the back half of it, then knit into the entire chain loop. Doing so will yield two stitches from one chain stitch, a technique I learned from lace knitters in Haapsalu, Estonia.

When the right or left side of the heel flap is mentioned, it refers to the right or left side as viewed when worn, not as a sock knitted from the top down is knitted.

The gussets are decreased every alternate round or every third round till reduced to the same number of stitches as are on the ankle.

I have always set up the stitches for working the gussets, as well as the toe shaping, so that the round begins at the back of the heel (as illustrated below), which I have always thought of as general convention. This arrangement puts half the heel stitches and the gusset stitches from the right side

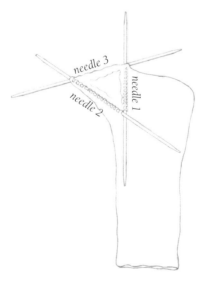

Arrange the stitches so that stitches for the right half of the heel and the right gusset are on needle 1, the instep stitches are on needle 2, and stitches for the left gusset and left half of the heel are on needle 3.

of the heel on needle 1, the instep stitches on needle 2 (or needles 2 and 3 if you're working with a set of 5 needles), and the left-side gusset stitches and the remaining heel stitches on needle 3 (or needle 4 if you're working with a set of 5 needles). The gusset decreases are worked at the end of the first needle and at the beginning of the last needle. However, a number of patterns in *Weldon's* don't follow this convention (Gentleman's Shooting Stockings on page 32, Gentleman's Sock in Railway Stitch on page 36, and Baby's Bootikin on page 92). Instead, the round begins after the instep stitches (and before the left gusset stitches). There is no explanation why the designers chose to do the gussets this way, but it works just as well and makes for a bit of variation in the knitting.

FINISHING

> Knit till the foot is the required length, then shape the toe, and cast off.

Many of the patterns throughout *Weldon's* give the instruction to do what we know as a three-needle bind-off to close the toe: "place the stitches onto two needles, hold them parallel and cast off by knitting a stitch from each needle at the same time." This rather unclear instruction yields a very bulky seam at the toe. In Volume 30 of *Weldon's Practical Knitter*, Ninety-ninth Series, from 1915, instructions are given for "Fastening off toes of Socks and Stockings by Grafting." This one-page article gives working instructions and detailed photographs of the process we know today as Kitchener stitch (Glossary, page 117) The text states that grafting "will prove a neat and strong

finish, and most comfortable in wear. The absence of a ridge of stitches or a point at the toe will commend the method to all knitters."

HEEL SHAPING

Weldon's offers a number of ways to shape a heel. Some are familiar favorites, others are more obscure. I have chosen the most interesting and accessible (taking into account needle sizes, yarn availability, and stitch count) and have rewritten the instructions for modern times. The instructions for each type of heel are written so that the technique can be used with any number of heel stitches, providing there are enough stitches to complete the heel turn. Each heel consists of three parts—a heel flap worked back and forth in rows, followed by a short-rowed heel turn, and finally gussets worked in the round with decreases to achieve the desired foot circumference. For the instructions given here, I follow the popular convention of beginning all rounds at the center back of the heel for shaping the gussets.

DUTCH OR HORSESHOE HEEL

The Dutch Heel is worked on half the total number of ankle stitches, plus one seam stitch. For example, if there are 64 stitches at the ankle, work the heel on 33 stitches. This type of heel is worked on the Madder Ribbed Sock (page 24).

Heel flap: Work the heel flap back and forth in rows in stockinette stitch, slipping (purlwise) the first stitch of every row to produce chain edge stitches along each selvedge, for as many rows as there are heel stitches. Work as follows:
Row 1: (RS) Knit a quarter of the total number of ankle sts beyond the seam st,

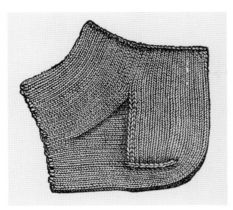

Dutch or Horseshoe Heel

German Heel

turn work. Note how many sts were worked beyond the seam st.

Row 2: Sl 1, purl to the seam st, purl the seam st, then purl as many more sts after the seam st as you noted above (the seam st will be in the center of the completed row), turn work—there will be half the total number of sts plus the seam st on one needle for the heel flap; the other half of the sts will be divided between two needles for the instep, which will be worked after the heel is completed.

Row 3: Sl 1, knit to the seam st, purl the seam st, knit to end.

Row 4: Sl 1, purl to the seam st, knit the seam st, purl to end.

Repeat Rows 3 and 4 until flap is the desired length.

Turn heel: Continue working the heel stitches in short rows as follows:

Row 1: (RS) Sl 1, knit to seam st, purl seam st, k5, sl 1, k1, psso, turn.

Row 2: Sl 1, p11, p2tog, turn.

Row 3: Sl 1, k5, p1 (seam st), k5, sl 1, k1, psso, turn.

Repeat Rows 2 and 3 until all heel sts have been worked, ending with a WS row.

Gussets: (RS) Knit across the heel stitches. With the same needle (needle 1) pick up and knit the desired number of stitches along right side of heel flap; with a new needle (needle 2), work across the instep stitches; with another new needle (needle 3), pick up and knit the stitches along left side of flap, then knit the first half of the heel sts again. The round begins at the center of the heel. Work decreases as follows:

Rnd 1: On needle 1, knit to the last 3 sts, k2tog, k1; on needle 2, knit across instep sts; on needle 3, k1, sl 1, k1, psso, knit to end of rnd—2 sts decreased.

Rnds 2 and 3: Knit all sts.

Repeat Rnds 1–3 until there remains the same number of stitches as there was at the ankle before the heel flap began.

GERMAN HEEL

This unusual heel is worked on half the total number of ankle stitches plus one seam stitch plus eight additional stitches (taken from the instep). For example, if there are 64 stitches at the ankle, work the heel on 41 stitches. The German Heel is worked on the Yarrow Ribbed Sock (page 28).

Heel flap: Work the heel flap back and forth in rows in stockinette stitch, slipping (purlwise) the first stitch of every row to produce chain edge stitches along each selvedge, for as many rows as there are heel stitches. Work as follows:

Row 1: (RS) Knit a quarter of the total number of ankle sts beyond the seam st, then p2, k2, turn work. Note how many sts are worked beyond the seam st.

Row 2: Sl 1, purl to the seam st, purl the seam st, then purl as many more sts after the seam st as you noted above (the seam st will be in the center of the completed row), turn work—the heel flap needle will have 9 more sts than half of the total number of ankle sts; the remaining sts will be divided between two needles for the instep, which will be worked after the heel is completed.

Row 3: Sl 1, k1, p2, knit to seam st, purl seam st, knit to last 4 sts, p2, k2, turn.

Row 4: Sl 1, purl to end.

Repeat Rows 3 and 4 until flap is desired length.

Turn heel: Continue working the heel sts in short rows as follows:

Row 1: (RS) Sl 1, k1, p2, knit to 3 sts past seam st (knit the seam st) sl 1, k1, psso, turn.

Row 2: (WS) Sl 1, p7, p2tog, turn.

Row 3: Sl 1, k8, sl 1, k1, psso, turn.

Repeat Rows 2 and 3, working 1 more stitch before the decrease in each row until all the heel stitches have been worked, ending with a WS row.

Gussets: Knit across the heel stitches, then with the same needle (needle 1), pick up and knit the desired number of stitches along the right side of the heel flap; with a new needle (needle 2) work across the instep sts; with another new needle (needle 3), pick up and knit the desired num-

ber of stitches along the left side of the heel flap, then work across half the heel stitches. The round begins at the center of the heel. Work decreases as follows:

Rnd 1: On needle 1, knit to the last 3 sts, p2tog, k1; on needle 2, work across instep sts; on needle 3, k1, p2tog, knit to end of rnd—2 sts decreased.

Rnd 2: Knit all sts.

Repeat Rnds 1–3 until there remains the same number of stitches as there was at the ankle, before the heel flap began.

WELSH HEEL

The Welsh Heel is shaped with decreases along the bottom of the heel. The result is "strong, but not perfectly smooth." It is worked on half the total number of ankle stitches plus one seam stitch; however, this type of heel works best if there are 30 or more stitches in the heel flap. For example, if there are 64 stitches at the ankle, work the heel on 33 stitches. This type of heel is worked on the Lichen Ribbed Sock (page 26).

Heel flap: Work the heel flap back and forth (in rows) in stockinette stitch, slipping (purlwise) the first stitch of every row to produce chain edge stitches along each selvedge, for as many rows as there are heel stitches. Work as follows:

Row 1: (RS) Knit a quarter of the total number of ankle sts beyond the seam st, turn work. Note how many sts were worked beyond the seam st.

Row 2: Sl 1, purl to the seam st, knit the seam st, then purl as many more sts after the seam st as you noted above (the seam st will be in the center of the completed row), turn work—there will be one st more than half the total number of ankle sts on the heel needle with the seam st in the center of the heel flap; the other half of the sts will be divided between two

Welsh Heel

French (Classic Round) Heel

needles for the instep, which will be worked after the heel is completed.

Row 3: Sl 1, knit to seam st, purl seam st, knit to end, turn.

Row 4: Sl 1, purl to seam st, knit seam st, purl to end.

Repeat Rows 3 and 4 until flap is the desired length.

Turn heel: Continue working the heel stitches in short rows as follows:

Row 1: (RS) Sl 1, knit to 10 before seam st, yo, k2tog, k5, k2tog, k1, p1 (seam st), k1, k2tog, k5, k2tog, turn.

Row 2: Yo, purl to seam st, k1 (seam st), purl to 10 sts past seam st, turn.

Row 3: Yo, k2tog, k5, k2tog, k1, p1 (seam st), k1, k2tog, k5, k2tog, turn.

Repeat Rows 2 and 3 until all heel stitches have been worked, omitting the starting yarnover (yo) in the last 2 rows, and ending with a WS row—17 stitches remain; 8 stitches on either side of seam stitch.

Gussets: Knit across the heel stitches, then with the same needle (needle 1), pick up and knit the desired number of stitches along the right side of the heel flap; with a new needle (needle 2), work across the instep stitches; with another new needle (needle 3), pick up and knit the desired number of stitches along the left side of the flap, then knit half the heel stitches again. The round begins at center of heel. Work decreases as follows:

Rnd 1: On needle 1, knit to the last 3 sts, k2tog, k1; on needle 2, knit across instep sts; on needle 3, k1, sl 1, k1, psso, knit to end of rnd—2 sts decreased.

Rnds 2 and 3: Knit all sts.

Repeat Rnds 1–3 until there remains the same number of stitches as there was at the ankle, before the heel flap began.

FRENCH (CLASSIC ROUND) HEEL

The popular French Heel is worked on half the total number of ankle stitches, plus 1 seam stitch. For example, if there are 64 stitches at the ankle, work the heel on 33 stitches. According to *Weldon's*, this type of heel is "especially suitable for a high instep." A French Heel or a variation of it is worked on the Oak Ribbed Sock (page 30).

Heel flap: Work the heel flap back and forth in rows in stockinette stitch, slipping (purlwise) the first stitch of every row to produce chain edge stitches along each selvedge, for as many rows as there are heel stitches. Work as follows:

Row 1: (RS) Knit a quarter of the total number of ankle sts beyond the seam st, turn work. Note how many sts were worked beyond the seam st.

Row 2: Sl 1, purl to the seam st, purl the seam st, then purl as many more sts after the seam st as you noted above (the seam st will be in the center of the completed row), turn work—there will be half the total number of sts plus the seam st on one needle for the heel flap; the other half of the sts will be divided between two needles for the instep, which will be worked after the heel is completed.

Row 3: Sl 1, knit to seam st, purl the seam st, knit to end.

Row 4: Sl 1, purl to seam st, knit the seam st, purl to end.

Repeat Rows 3 and 4 until flap is the desired length.

Turn heel: Continue working the heel stitches in short rows as follows:

Row 1: (RS) Sl 1, knit to seam st, k2 (the seam st plus the next st), sl 1, k1, psso, k1, turn.

Row 2: Sl 1, p4, p2tog, p1, turn.

Row 3: Sl 1, k5, sl 1, k1, psso, k1, turn.

Row 4: Sl 1, p6, p2tog, p1, turn.

Row 5: Sl 1, k7, sl 1, k1, psso, k1, turn.

Row 6: Sl 1, p8, p2tog, p1, turn.

Continue as established, working 1 more stitch before the decrease every row until all of the stitches have been worked, ending with a WS row.

Gussets: Knit across the heel stitches, then with the same needle (needle 1), pick up and knit the desired number of stitches along the right side of the flap; with a new needle (needle 2), work across the instep stitches; with another

new needle (needle 3), pick up and knit the desired number of stitches along the left side of the flap, then knit half the heel stitches again. The round begins at center of heel. Work decreases as follows:

Rnd 1: On needle 1, knit to the last 3 sts, k2tog, k1; on needle 2, work across instep sts; on needle 3, k1, sl 1, k1, psso, knit to end of rnd—2 sts decreased.

Rnds 2 and 3: Knit all sts.

Repeat Rnds 1–3 until there remains the same number of stitches as there was at the ankle, before the heel flap began.

TOE SHAPING

Weldon's offers a number of ways to finish off a sock toe. Below are six examples, many of which are commonly used today. These instructions follow the convention of beginning all rounds at the center sole of the foot.

ROUND TOE

The Round Toe is worked over a relatively large number of rounds. To keep the sock from being too long, you'll want to work fewer rounds in the foot before you begin this toe. A Round Toe is worked on the Oak Ribbed Stocking (page 30).

This toe is begun on a number of stitches divisible by 10, arranged so that half of the stitches are on the instep needle (needle 2) and the other half of the stitches are evenly divided between two sole needles (needles 1 and 3). Decrease as follows:

Rnd 1: *K8, k2tog; rep from * to end.

Rnds 2–9: Knit.

Rnd 10: *K7, k2tog; rep from * to end.

Rnds 11–17: Knit.

Continue in this manner, knitting 1 less stitch between decreases on decrease rounds, and working 1 less round between decrease rounds until you've worked a round consisting of all k2togs. According to *Weldon's*, the proper way to finish off the

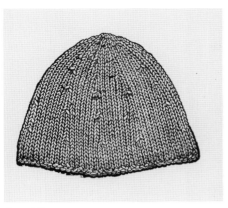

Round Toe

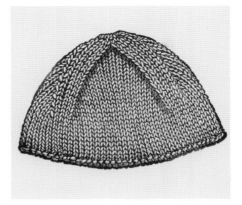

French Toe

Round Toe is to "cast off all sts." However, I prefer to avoid the bulky seam by cutting the yarn, threading the tail on a tapestry needle, drawing the needle through all the stitches, then pulling tight to close the opening (Glossary, page 117).

Note: A Round Toe can be shortened by working it over a number of stitches divisible by 8 (making the first decrease round k6, k2tog), and working fewer rounds between decrease rounds, as is done for the Heelless Sleeping Socks (page 52), Gentleman's Half Hose in Ringwood Pattern (page 64), and Evening Stockings for a Young Lady (page 72).

FRENCH TOE

A French Toe is worked over a relatively few number of rounds; work the foot for a few more rounds before you begin this type of toe. This toe is used on the Yarrow Ribbed Sock (page 28).

Begin by dividing the stitches equally among 3 needles so that the center stitch of the bottom of the foot is the first stitch on needle 1. Decrease as follows:
Rnd 1: On needle 1, *k1, sl 1, k1, psso, knit to last 3 sts on needle, k2tog, k1; rep from * for needles 2 and 3—6 sts decreased.
Rnd 2: Knit.
Repeat Rnds 1 and 2 until 12 stitches

remain. According to *Weldon's*, you should then "cast off all sts." Again, I prefer to avoid the bulky seam by cutting the yarn, threading the tail on a tapestry needle, drawing the needle through all the stitches, then pulling tight to close the opening (Glossary, page 117).

POINTED TOE

A Pointed Toe is best worked on a number of stitches divisible by 4, which is the number of stitches that's eliminated every decrease round. The result is a serpentine pattern that spirals around the tip of the foot. The example in *Weldon's* begins with 76 stitches. If you want to use this shaping on a sock with just 60 stitches, as for the Madder Ribbed Sock (page 24), follow the instructions below, but begin with Rnd 16.

Begin by dividing the stitches equally among 3 needles so that the center stitch of the bottom of the foot is the first stitch on needle 1. The round begins at the bottom of the foot. Decrease as follows:
Rnd 1: *K7, sl 1, k1, psso, k10; rep from *.
Rnds 2–4: Knit.
Rnd 5: *K7, sl 1, k1, psso, k9; rep from *.
Rnds 6–8: Knit.
Rnd 9: *K7, sl 1, k1, psso, k8; rep from *.
Rnds 10–12: Knit.

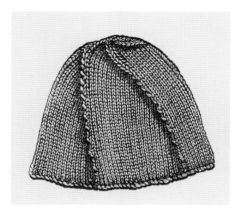

Pointed Toe

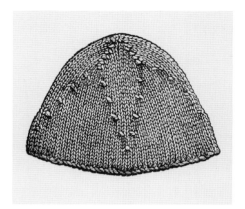

Star Toe of Four Points

Rnd 13: *K7, sl 1, k1, psso, k7; rep from *.
Rnds 14 and 15: Knit.
Rnd 16: *K7, sl 1, k1, psso, k6; rep from *.
Rnds 17 and 18: Knit.
Rnd 19: *K7, sl 1, k1, psso, k5; rep from *.
Rnds 20 and 21: Knit.
Rnd 22: *K7, sl 1, k1, psso, k4; rep from *.
Rnds 23, 25, 27, and 29: Knit.
Rnd 24: *K7, sl 1, k1, psso, k3; rep from *.
Rnd 26: *K7, sl 1, k1, psso, k2; rep from *.
Rnd 28: *K7, sl 1, k1, psso, k1; rep from *.
Rnd 30: *K7, sl 1, k1, psso; rep from *.
Rnd 31: *K6, sl 1 k1, psso; rep from *.
From this point on, decrease every round, working 1 stitch less between decreases, until 4 stitches remain. Cut yarn, thread tail on a tapestry needle, draw the needle through all the stitches, and pull tight to close the opening (Glossary, page 117).

STAR TOE OF THREE POINTS

This toe is a variation of two toes offered in *Weldon's*: the Star Toe of Four Points and the Star Toe of Five Points. Each of these toes requires 80 sts to begin with. Because few knitters will work at that tiny a gauge, I have revised the instructions to be worked over a smaller number of stitches. I call my variation Star Toe of Three Points. This type of toe is used for the Lichen Ribbed Sock (page 26).

Begin with 60 stitches. Arrange the stitches on three needles with 20 stitches on each needle. The round begins at the bottom of the foot. Decrease as follows:
Rnd 1: *K19, p1; rep from *.
Rnds 2–5: Knit.
Rnd 6: *P2tog, k15, p2tog, k1; rep from *—54 sts rem.
Rnds 7–10: Knit.
Rnd 11: *K1, p2tog, k11, p2tog, k2; rep from *—48 sts rem.
Rnds 12–15: Knit.
Rnd 16: *K2, p2tog, k7, p2tog, k3; rep from *—42 sts rem.
Rnds 17–20: Knit.
Rnd 21: *K3, p2tog, k3, p2tog, k4; rep from *—36 sts rem.
Rnds 22–25: Knit.
Rnd 26: *K4, p3tog, k5; rep from *—30 sts rem.
Rnd 27: *K3, p3tog, k4; rep from *—24 sts rem.
Rnd 28: *K2, p3tog, k3; rep from *—18 sts rem.
Rnd 29: *K1, p3tog, k2; rep from *—12 sts rem.
Rnd 30: *P3tog, k1; rep from *—6 sts rem.
Cut yarn, thread tail on a tapestry needle,

Flat Toe

Wide Toe

draw the needle through all the stitches, and pull tight to close the opening (Glossary, page 117).

FLAT TOE

A Flat Toe can be worked on any number of stitches divisible by 4, which is the number of stitches that's eliminated every decrease round. This popular toe is used on many of the socks in this book.

Begin by arranging the stitches so that half of the stitches are on the instep needle (needle 2) and the other half of the stitches are evenly divided between two sole needles (needles 1 and 3). The round begins at the bottom of the foot. Decrease as follows:

Rnd 1: On needle 1, knit to the last 3 sts, k2tog, k1; on needle 2, k1, sl 1, k1, psso, knit to the last 3 sts, k2tog, k1; on needle 3, k1, sl 1, k1, psso, knit to end.

Rnd 2: Knit.

Repeat Rnds 1 and 2 until 24 stitches remain (12 on the instep needle and 6 on each of the back needles). The instructions in *Weldon's* say to finish off with a three-needle bind-off. I prefer to use the

Kitchener stitch (Glossary, page 117) to reduce bulk.

WIDE TOE

A Wide Toe is similar to a Flat Toe, but there are more stitches between the decreases at each side of the foot.

Begin by arranging the stitches so that half of the stitches are on the instep needle (needle 2) and the other half of the stitches are evenly divided between two sole needles (needles 1 and 3). The round begins at the bottom of the foot. Decrease as follows:

Rnd 1: On needle 1, knit to last 6 sts, k2tog, k4; on needle 2, k4, sl 1, k1, psso, knit to last 6 sts, k2tog, k4; on needle 3, k4, sl 1, k1, psso, knit to end—4 sts decreased.

Rnds 2–4: Knit.

Repeat Rnds 1–4 once, then work Rnds 1–3 three times, then repeat Rnds 1 and 2 until 28 stitches remain. The instructions in *Weldon's* say to finish off with a three-needle bind-off. However, I prefer to end this toe with the Kitchener stitch (Glossary, page 117).

SIMPLE RIBBED SOCKS

Weldon's is filled with solid-colored stocking and sock patterns that have ribbing down the leg and often onto the foot. I have chosen to offer four variations of ribbed socks, all with a different rib pattern, to illustrate some of the more interesting ribbings and heel and toe shapings used in *Weldon's*.

MADDER RIBBED SOCK

This ribbed sock has a Dutch or Horseshoe Heel and a Pointed Toe. The heel is similar to a Square Heel, and the toe is a variation on the Star Toe from my first book, *Folk Socks* (Interweave Press, 1994). *Weldon's* offers a different style of Star Toe. I have rewritten the instructions for the heel and toe shaping to get the same results as in *Weldon's*.

Madder Ribbed Sock

SPECIFICATIONS

Finished Size 7½" (19 cm) foot circumference, 8" (20.5 cm) long from cast-on edge to top of heel flap, and 9½" (24 cm) long from back of heel to tip of toe. To fit women's U.S. shoe sizes 8 to 9.

Yarn About 350 yd (320 m) of fingering-weight (Super-Fine #1) yarn. We used Wooly West Footpath (85% wool, 15% nylon; 175 yd [160 m]/2 oz; 18 wraps per inch): madder, 2 skeins.

Needles Size 1 (2.5 mm): set of 4 double-pointed. Adjust needle size if necessary to obtain the correct gauge.

Notions Stitch marker (m); tapestry needle.

Gauge 15 sts and 20 rnds = 2" (5 cm) in St st worked in the rnd, before blocking.

LEG

CO 60 sts. Divide sts evenly onto 3 needles (20 sts on each needle). Join for working in the rnd, being careful not to twist sts, and place marker (pm) after first st to denote beg of rnd.

Cuff: Work k2, p2 ribbing for 16 rnds—piece should measure 1½" (3.8 cm) from beg.

Leg: K1, p1, *k6, p1, k2, p1; rep from * to last 8 sts, k6, p1, k1. Rep this rnd until piece measures 8" (20.5 cm) from CO.

HEEL

Heel flap: Set up for working heel sts on 1 needle as foll: M1 (Glossary, page 115), k15, turn work, sl 1, p14, k1, p15—31 sts on the heel needle; center st is the "seam" st at center of heel. Hold rem 30 sts on 2 needles to be worked later for instep. Work 31 heel sts back and forth in rows as foll:

Row 1: (RS) Sl 1, k14, p1, k15.

Row 2: (WS) Sl 1, p14, k1, p15.

Rep Rows 1 and 2 until a total of 30 rows have been worked—15 chain sts (slipped selvedge sts) along each edge of heel flap.

Turn heel: Work in short rows as foll:

Row 1: (RS) Sl 1, k14, p1, k5, sl 1, k1, psso, turn.

Row 2: (WS) Sl 1, p11, p2tog, turn.

Row 3: Sl 1, k5, p1, k5, sl 1, k1, psso, turn.

Rep Rows 2 and 3 until all heel sts have been worked, ending with Row 2; the seam st will be purled every row to form a garter-stitch column—13 heel sts rem.

Gussets: Rejoin for working in the rnd as foll:

Rnd 1: With needle 1, work 13 heel sts as foll: k6, k2tog, k5, then pick up and knit 16 sts along right side of heel flap; with needle 2, work 30 instep sts in established

rib; with needle 3, pick up and knit 16 sts along left side of heel flap, then knit the first 6 sts from needle 1 again—74 sts total; 22 heel sts each on needles 1 and 3, 30 instep sts on needle 2.

Rnd 2: On needle 1, knit to last 3 sts, k2tog, k1; on needle 2, work 30 instep sts as established; on needle 3, k1, sl 1, k1, psso, knit to end—72 sts.

Rnds 3 and 4: Work even as established (knit heel sts; work instep sts in rib).

Rnd 5: On needle 1, knit to last 3 sts, k2tog, k1; on needle 2, work instep sts as established; on needle 3, k1, sl 1, k1, psso, knit to end—2 sts dec'd.

Rep Rnds 3–5 until 60 sts rem—15 sts each on needles 1 and 2, 30 instep sts on needle 3.

FOOT

Cont in patt as established until foot measures 6" (15 cm) from back of heel, or 3½" (9 cm) less than desired total length.

TOE

Rnd 1: *K3, sl 1, k1, psso, k10; rep from *—56 sts rem.

Rnds 2–4: Knit.

Rnd 5: *K3, sl 1, k1, psso, k9; rep from *—52 sts rem.

Rnds 6–8: Knit.

Rnd 9: *K3, sl 1, k1, psso, k8; rep from *—48 sts rem.

Rnds 10–12: Knit.

Rnd 13: *K3, sl 1, k1, psso, k7; rep from *—44 sts rem.

Rnds 14 and 15: Knit.

Rnd 16: *K3, sl 1, k1, psso, k6; rep from *—40 sts rem.

Rnds 17 and 18: Knit.

Rnd 19: *K3, sl 1, k1, psso, k5; rep from *—36 sts rem.

Rnds 20 and 21: Knit.

Rnd 22: *K3, sl 1, k1, psso, k4; rep from *—32 sts rem.

Rnd 23: Knit.

Rnd 24: *K3, sl 1, k1, psso, k3; rep from *—28 sts rem.

Rnd 25: Knit.

Rnd 26: *K3, sl 1, k1, psso, k2; rep from *—24 sts rem.

Rnd 27: Knit.

Rnd 28: *K3, sl 1, k1, psso, k1; rep from *—20 sts rem.

Rnd 29: Knit.

Rnd 30: *K3, sl 1, k1, psso; rep from *—16 sts rem.

Rnd 31: *K2, sl 1, k1, psso; rep from *—12 sts rem.

Rnd 32: *K1, sl 1, k1, psso; rep from *—8 sts rem.

Rnd 33: *Sl 1, k1, psso; rep from *—4 sts rem.

Cut yarn. Thread tail on a tapestry needle, draw tail through rem sts, and pull up snugly to close end of toe. Weave in loose ends. Block on sock blockers or under a damp towel.

LICHEN RIBBED SOCK

This stocking is a shortened version of the Cycling or Golf Stockings with Fancy Cuff in Trellis Pattern shown on page 48. It has a Welsh Heel and a Star Toe of Three Points.

LEG

With MC, CO 60 sts. Divide sts evenly onto 3 needles (20 sts each needle). Join for working in the rnd, being careful not to twist sts, and place marker (pm) after first st to denote beg of rnd.

Cuff: Work k1, p1 ribbing for 16 rnds—piece should measure 1½" (3.8 cm) from beg.

Leg: *K3, p1; rep from * to end. Rep this rnd until leg measures 8½" (21.5 cm) from beg.

SPECIFICATIONS

Finished Size 7½" (19 cm) foot circumference, 8½" (21.5 cm) long from cast-on edge to top of heel flap, and 9½" (24 cm) long from back of heel to tip of toe. To fit women's U.S. shoe sizes 8 to 9.

Yarn About 350 yd (320 m) of fingering-weight (Super-Fine #1) yarn. We used Wooly West Footpath (85% wool, 15% nylon; 175 yd [160 m]/ 2 oz; 18 wraps per inch) lichen, 2 skeins.

Needles Size 1 (2.5 mm): set of 4 double-pointed. Adjust needle size if necessary to obtain the correct length.

Notions Stitch marker (m); tapestry needle.

Gauge 15 sts and 20 rnds = 2" (5 cm) in St st worked in the rnd, before blocking.

HEEL

Heel flap: Set up for working heel sts on 1 needle as foll: K15, turn, sl 1, p14, k1 ("seam" st), p15—31 sts on heel needle. Place rem 29 sts on 2 needles to be worked later for instep (first and last sts of instep should be purl sts). Work 31 heel sts back and forth in rows as foll:

Row 1: (RS) Sl 1, k14, p1 (seam st), k15.

Row 2: (WS) Sl 1, p14, k1, p15.

Rep Rows 1 and 2 fifteen times total—30 heel flap rows, ending with a WS row; 15 chain sts (slipped selvedge sts) along each edge of heel flap.

Turn heel: Work short rows as foll (the yarnovers will form very small holes at each turn):

Row 1: (RS) *Sl 1, k4, yo, k2tog, k5, k2tog, k1, p1 (seam st), k1, k2tog, k5, k2tog, turn.

Row 2: (WS) Yo, purl to seam st, k1 (seam st), purl to 10 sts beyond seam st (purling yo of previous row, and counting it as 1 purl st), turn.

Row 3: Yo, k2tog, k5, k2tog, k1, p1 (seam st), k1, k2tog, k5, k2tog (yo of previous row and next st), turn.

Rep Rows 2 and 3 four more times; decs on either side of seam st will not be symmetrical mirror images of each other—18 sts (including yo).

Row 4: (WS) Sl 1, purl to seam st, k1 (seam st), purl to last 2 sts, p2tog—17 sts; 8 sts on either side of seam st.

Gussets: Rejoin for working in the rnd as foll:

Rnd 1: With RS facing and needle 1, knit across 17 heel sts, pick up and knit 15 sts along right side of heel flap; with needle 2, work across 29 instep sts in established rib; with needle 3, pick up and knit 15 sts along left side of heel flap, then knit the first 9 sts from needle 1 again—76 sts total; 23 sts on needle 1, 29 instep sts on needle 2, 24 sts on needle 3. Rnd begins at center of heel.

Rnd 2: On needle 1, knit to last 3 sts, k2tog, k1; on needle 2, work sts as they appear (knit the knits and purl the purls); on needle 3, k1, sl 1, k1, psso, knit to end—74 sts; 22 sts on needle 1, 29 instep sts on needle 2, 23 sts on needle 3.

Rnd 3: Work even as established.

Rnd 4: On needle 1, knit to last 3 sts, k2tog, k1; on needle 2, work even in patt; on needle 3, k1, sl 1, k1, psso, knit to end—2 sts dec'd.

Rep Rnds 3 and 4 six more times—60 sts rem; 16 sts on needle 1, 15 sts on needle 3, 29 instep sts on needle 2.

FOOT

Cont in patt as established until foot measures 6½" (16.5 cm) from back of heel, or 3" (7.5 cm) less than desired total length, ending 4 sts before the end of the last rnd.

Lichen Ribbed Sock

TOE

Arrange sts so that there are 20 sts on each needle by placing the first 5 instep sts onto needle 2, and the last 4 instep sts onto needle 1.

Rnd 1: *K19, p1; rep from *.

Rnds 2–5: Knit.

Rnd 6: *P2tog, k15, p2tog, k1; rep from *—54 sts rem.

Rnds 7–10: Knit.

Rnd 11: *K1, p2tog, k11, p2tog, k2; rep from *—48 sts rem.

Rnds 12–15: Knit.

Rnd 16: *K2, p2tog, k7, p2tog, k3; rep from *—42 sts rem.

Rnds 17–20: Knit.

Rnd 21: *K3, p2tog, k3, p2tog, k4; rep from *—36 sts rem.

Rnds 22–25: Knit.

Rnd 26: *K4, p3tog, k5; rep from *—30 sts rem.

Rnd 27: *K3, p3tog, k4; rep from *—24 sts rem.

Rnd 28: *K2, p3tog, k3; rep from *—18 sts rem.

Rnd 29: *K1, p3tog, k2; rep from *—12 sts rem.

Rnd 30: *P3tog, k1; rep from *—6 sts rem. Cut yarn, leaving a 12" (30.5-cm) tail. Thread tail on a tapestry needle, draw tail through rem sts, and pull up snugly to close end of toe. Weave in loose ends. Block on sock blockers or under a damp towel.

YARROW RIBBED SOCK

I've designed this stocking with another rib pattern adapted from the pages of *Weldon's*. It has a German Heel and a French Toe.

LEG

CO 66 sts. Divide sts evenly onto 3 needles (22 sts each needle). Join, being care-

SPECIFICATIONS

Finished Size 8" (20.5 cm) foot circumference, 8½" (21.5 cm) long from cast-on edge to top of heel flap, and 9½" (24 cm) long from back of heel to tip of toe. To fit women's U.S. shoe sizes 8 to 9.
Yarn About 350 yd (320 m) of fingering-weight (Super Fine #1) yarn. We used Wooly West Footpath (85% wool, 15% nylon; 175 yd [160 m]/2 oz; 18 wraps per inch): yarrow, 2 skeins.
Needles Size 1 (2.5 mm): set of 4 double-pointed. Adjust needle size if necessary to obtain the correct gauge.
Notions Stitch marker (m); tapestry needle.
Gauge 15 sts and 20 rnds = 2" (5 cm) in St st worked in the rnd, before blocking.

ful not to twist sts, and place marker (pm) after first st to denote beg of rnd.

Cuff: *P1, k1, p1, k3; rep from * to end of rnd. Rep this rnd 15 more times—piece should measure 1½" (3.8 cm) from beg.

Leg: *K3, p1, k1, p1; rep from * to end of rnd. Rep this rnd until piece measures 8½" (21.5 cm) from CO.

HEEL

Heel flap: Set up for working heel sts on 1 needle as foll: K18, turn, sl 1, p18, p1 ("seam" st), p19—39 sts. Hold rem 27 sts on 2 needles to be worked later for instep. Work 39 heel sts back and forth in rows as foll:

Row 1: (RS) Sl 1, k1, p2, k15, p1 (seam st), k15, p2, k2.

Row 2: (WS) Sl 1, purl to end.

Rep Rows 1 and 2 rows until a total of 30 rows have been worked, ending with a WS row—15 chain sts (slipped selvedge sts) along each edge of heel flap.

Turn heel: Work in short rows as foll:

Row 1: (RS) Sl 1, k1, p2, k15, k1 (seam st), k3, sl 1, k1, psso, turn.

Row 2: (WS) Sl 1, p7, p2tog, turn.

Row 3: Sl 1, k8, sl 1, k1, psso, turn.

Row 4: Sl 1, p9, p2tog, turn.

Row 5: Sl 1, k10, sl 1, k1, psso, turn.

Row 6: Sl 1, p11, p2tog, turn.

Cont in this manner, working 1 more st before the dec each row until all sts have been worked, ending with a WS row—23 heel sts rem.

Gussets: Rejoin for working in the rnd as foll:

Rnd 1: With needle 1, knit across 23 heel sts, then pick up and knit 15 sts along right side of heel flap; with needle 2, work 27 instep sts in established rib patt; with needle 3, pick up and knit 15 sts along left side of heel, then knit the first 12 sts from needle 1 again—80 sts total; 26 heel sts on needle 1, 27 instep sts on needle 2, 27 heel sts on needle 3. Rnd begins at center of heel.

Rnd 2: On needle 1, knit to last 3 sts, p2tog, k1; on needle 2, work 27 instep sts as established; on needle 3, k1, p2tog, knit to end—2 sts dec'd.

Rnd 3: Work even in patt as established.

Rep Rnds 2 and 3 until 66 sts rem—19 sts on needle 1, 27 instep sts on needle 2, 20 sts on needle 3.

FOOT

Cont in patt as established until foot measures 7" (18 cm) from back of heel, or 2½" (6.5 cm) less than desired total length. Knit all sts for 5 rnds, rearranging sts evenly with 22 sts on each needle in last rnd.

TOE

Rnd 1: K1, sl 1, k1, psso, knit to last 3 sts on needle, k2tog, k1; rep from * for next 2 needles—6 sts dec'd.

Rnd 2: Knit.

Rep Rnds 1 and 2 until 12 sts rem—4 sts each on three needles. Cut yarn. Thread tail on a tapestry needle, draw tail through rem sts, and pull up snugly to close end of toe. Weave in loose ends. Block on sock blockers or under a damp towel.

Yarrow Ribbed Sock

OAK RIBBED SOCK

This ribbed sock has a French Heel and a Round Toe. The French heel is the same as the Round Heel I used in *Folk Socks* (Interweave Press, 1994). I modified the Round Toe shaping from that shown in *Weldon's* (the original is worked on a multiple of 10 stitches and is worked over 45 rounds). The toe in this version is worked over a multiple of 8 stitches and requires just 28 rounds.

LEG

CO 63 sts. Divide sts evenly onto 3 needles (21 sts each needle). Join, being careful not to twist sts, and place marker (pm) after first st to denote beg of rnd.

Cuff: *K1, p2, k2, p2; rep from * to end of rnd. Rep this rnd 15 more times—piece should measure 1½" (3.8 cm) from beg.

Leg: *K1, p1, k4, p1; rep from * to end of rnd. Rep this rnd until piece measures 7½" (19 cm) from CO.

HEEL

Heel flap: Set up for working heel sts on 1 needle as foll: K16, turn, sl 1, p15, k1 ("seam" st), p16—33 sts. Hold rem 30 sts on 2 needles to be worked later for instep. Work 33 heel sts back and forth in rows as foll:

Row 1: (RS) Sl 1, k15, p1, k16.
Row 2: (WS) Sl 1, p15, k1, p16.

Rep Rows 1 and 2 until a total of 32 rows have been worked, ending with a WS row—16 chain sts (slipped selvedge sts) along each edge of heel flap.

Turn heel: Work in short rows as foll:

Row 1: (RS) Sl 1, k15, p1 (seam st), k1, sl 1, k1, psso, k1, turn.
Row 2: (WS) Sl 1, p4, p2tog, p1, turn.
Row 3: Sl 1, k5, sl 1, k1, psso, k1, turn.
Row 4: Sl 1, p6, p2tog, p1, turn.
Row 5: Sl 1, k7, sl 1, k1, psso, k1, turn.
Row 6: Sl 1, p8, p2tog, p1, turn.

Cont in this manner, working 1 more st before the dec each row until all heel sts have been worked, working seam st in St st, and ending with a WS row—19 heel sts rem.

Gussets: Rejoin for working in the rnd as foll:

Rnd 1: With needle 1, knit across 19 heel sts, then pick up and knit 16 sts along right side of heel flap; with needle 2, work 30 instep sts in established rib patt; with needle 3, pick up and knit 16 sts along left side of heel, then knit the first 9 sts from needle 1 again—81 sts total; 26 sts on needle 1, 30 instep sts on needle 2, 25 sts on needle 3. Rnd begins at center of heel.

SPECIFICATIONS

Finished Size 7¾" (19.5 cm) foot circumference, 7½" (19 cm) long from cast-on edge to top of heel flap, and 9½" (24 cm) long from back of heel to tip of toe. To fit women's U.S. shoe sizes 8 to 9.

Yarn About 350 yd (320 m) of fingering-weight (Super Fine #1) yarn. We used Wooly West Footpath (85% wool, 15% nylon; 175 yd [160 m]/2 oz; 18 wraps per inch): oak, 2 skeins.

Needles Size 1 (2.5 mm): set of 4 double-pointed. Adjust needle size if necessary to obtain the correct gauge.

Notions Stitch marker (m); tapestry needle.

Gauge 15 sts and 20 rnds = 2" (5 cm) in St st worked in the rnd, before blocking.

Rnd 2: On needle 1, knit to last 3 sts, k2tog, k1; on needle 2, work 30 instep sts as established; on needle 3, k1, sl 1, k1, psso, knit to end—2 sts dec'd.

Rnds 3 and 4: Work even as established (knit heel sts work instep sts in rib patt).

Rnd 5: On needle 1, knit to last 3 sts, k2tog, k1; on needle 2, work instep sts as established; on needle 3, k1, sl 1, k1, psso, knit to end—2 sts dec'd.

Rep Rnds 3–5 until 65 sts rem—18 sts on needle 1, 30 instep sts on needle 2, 17 sts on needle 3. Rep Rnds 3 and 4 once more.

Next rnd: On needle 1, knit to last 3 sts, k2tog, k1; on needle 2, work instep sts as established; on needle 3, knit to end—64 sts rem; 17 sts each on needles 1 and 3, 30 instep sts on needle 2.

FOOT

Cont in patt as established until foot measures 7" (18 cm) from back of heel, or 2½" (6.5 cm) less than desired total length.

TOE

Rnd 1: *K6, k2tog; rep from *—56 sts rem.

Rnds 2–7: Knit.

Rnd 8: *K5, k2tog; rep from *—48 sts rem.

Rnds 9–13: Knit.

Rnd 14: *K4, k2tog; rep from *—40 sts rem.

Rnds 15–18: Knit.

Rnd 19: *K3, k2tog; rep from *—32 sts rem.

Rnds 20–22: Knit.

Rnd 23: *K2, k2tog; rep from *—24 sts rem.

Rnds 24 and 25: Knit.

Rnd 26: *K1, k2tog; rep from *—16 sts rem.

Rnd 27: Knit.

Rnd 28: *K2tog; rep from *—8 sts rem. Cut yarn. *Weldon's* says to bind off all sts when toe is completed, but I prefer to thread the tail on a tapestry needle, draw tail through rem sts, and pull up snugly to close end of toe. Weave in loose ends. Block on sock blockers or under a damp towel.

Oak Ribbed Sock

GENTLEMAN'S SHOOTING STOCKINGS

with Fluted Pattern

Weldon's, Volume 2, Fifth Series, 1887, page 10

Original specified 9 ounces of 5-ply Scotch Fingering; four #15 (U.S. 000; 1.5 mm) needles.

These Gentleman's Shooting Stockings are an abbreviation of the stocking offered in *Weldon's*. The original came up to the knee, perhaps even over it, and was meant to be worn with knickerbockers. The construction of this stocking is a bit unusual because the seam stitch at the back of the leg is not centered at the join of the rounds, but is placed at the end of the first needle. Also, the gusset shaping for the foot begins on what we usually think of as the last needle; here, that needle has become needle 1. I have followed the French Heel as specified in the original pattern, but instead of ending the Flat Toe shaping with a three-needle bind-off, I have worked a Kitchener stitch for a smooth finish. And although the original pattern calls for working on a set of four needles, I have worked on five.

SPECIFICATIONS

Finished Size 8" (20.5 cm) foot circumference, 10" (25.5 cm) long from cast-on edge to top of heel flap, and 10" (25.5 cm) long from back of heel to tip of toe. To fit men's U.S. shoe sizes 8 to 9.
Yarn About 600 yd (549 m) of fingering-weight (Super Fine #1) yarn. We used Sunbeam St. Ives (80% wool, 20% nylon; 200 yd [182 m]/50 g; 19 wraps per inch): #3107 mallard, 3 skeins.
Needles Size 0 (2 mm): set of 5 double-pointed. Adjust needle size if necessary to obtain the correct gauge.
Notions Stitch marker (m); removable stitch marker or safety pin; tapestry needle.
Gauge 17 sts and 22 rnds = 2" (5 cm) in St st worked in the rnd, before blocking.

LEG

CO 84 sts onto 1 needle. Divide sts onto 4 needles so that there are 24 sts each on needles 1 and 2, and 18 sts each on needles 3 and 4. Join for working in the rnd, being careful not to twist sts, and place marker (pm) after first st to denote beg of rnd.

Cuff: Work k3, p3 ribbing for 35 rnds—piece should measure 3" (7.5 cm) from beg.
Leg: Work Rnds 1–5 of written instructions for fluted patt (page 35) 6 times—piece should measure 5¼" (13.5 cm) from beg. *Next rnd:* Beg Rnd 1 of chart, work the sts on needles 1 and 2 according to Leg Shaping chart (page 35), keeping in established patt on needles 3 and 4. With removable stitch marker or safety pin, mark the last st of needle 1 for the "seam" st as indicated on chart; move marker up every few rnds as you work. After completing Rnd 26 of chart, 72 sts rem. Cont as established until Rnd 30 of chart has been completed—18 sts on each needle. Cont even in patt until piece measures about 10" (25.5 cm) from beg, or desired length to top of heel, ending with Rnd 5 of patt.

HEEL

Heel flap: Work in patt to seam st, purl seam st, then with same needle, work 18 more sts in patt—36 sts on needle for heel. Hold rem 36 sts on 2 needles to be worked later for instep. Work 36 heel sts back and forth in rows as foll:
Row 1: (WS) Sl 1, work 35 sts in patt.
Row 2: (RS) Sl 1, work 35 sts in patt.
Rep Rows 1 and 2 until a total of 34 heel rows have been worked (6 full 5-row patt reps, plus the first 4 rows of the 7th rep), ending with a WS row—17 chain sts (slipped selvedge sts) along each edge of heel flap.
Turn heel: Work short rows as foll:
Row 1: (RS) Sl 1, k18, sl 1, k1, psso, k1, turn.
Row 2: (WS) Sl 1, p3, p2tog, p1, turn.
Row 3: Sl 1, knit to 1 st before gap made on previous row, sl 1, k1, psso, k1, turn.
Row 4: Sl 1, purl to 1 st before gap made on previous row, p2tog, p1, turn.
Rep Rows 3 and 4 until all heel sts have been worked, ending with Row 4—20 heel sts rem.
Gussets: Rejoin for working in the rnd as foll:
Rnd 1: With one needle (this will become needle 2), k20 heel sts, then pick up and knit 18 sts along right side of heel flap; with another needle (this will become needle 3), work 36 instep sts in patt as established; with

Safety pin invented	Domestic sewing machine patented	Queen Victoria administered chloroform	Typewriter patented	Charles Dickens publishes *A Tale of Two Cities*	Commercial baby food launched in Germany	Saccharine discovered	Indigo synthesized in Germany	Male farm laborers and domestics able to vote	First motor cars	26,000 homes in U.K. have a telephone	Eastman Kodak camera available in U.S.
1849	1851	1853	1854	1859	1867	1879	1880	1884	1885	1887	1888

Leg Shaping

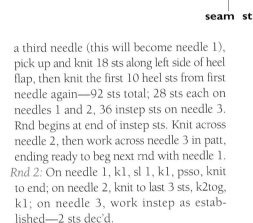

☐	knit	
⊡	purl	
⁄	k2tog	
⟍	sl 1, k1, psso	
⟋	p2tog	
▨	no stitch	

29
27
25
23
21
19
17
15
13
11
9
7
5
3
1

↑
seam st

a third needle (this will become needle 1), pick up and knit 18 sts along left side of heel flap, then knit the first 10 heel sts from first needle again—92 sts total; 28 sts each on needles 1 and 2, 36 instep sts on needle 3. Rnd begins at end of instep sts. Knit across needle 2, then work across needle 3 in patt, ending ready to beg next rnd with needle 1.

Rnd 2: On needle 1, k1, sl 1, k1, psso, knit to end; on needle 2, knit to last 3 sts, k2tog, k1; on needle 3, work instep as established—2 sts dec'd.

Rnds 3 and 4: Work even in patt.

Rep Rnds 2–4 ten more times—70 sts rem; 17 sts each on needles 1 and 2, 36 instep sts on needle 3.

FOOT

Cont in patt as established until foot measures 7½" (19 cm) from back of heel, or 2½" (6.5 cm) less than desired total length, ending with Rnd 5 of fluted patt on instep sts.

TOE

Rnd 1: On needle 1, k1, sl 1, k1, psso, knit to end; on needle 2, knit to last 3 sts, k2tog, k1; on needle 3, k1, sl 1, k1, psso, k7, k2tog, k10, k2tog, k9, k2tog, k1—64 sts rem.

Rnd 2: Knit.

Rnd 3: On needle 1, k1, sl 1, k1, psso, knit to end; on needle 2, knit to last 3 sts, k2tog, k1; on needle 3, k1, sl 1, k1, psso, knit to last 3 sts, k2 tog, k1—4 sts dec'd.

Rep Rnds 2 and 3 nine more times—24 sts rem; 6 sts each on needles 1 and 2, 12 instep sts on needle 3. Sl sts from needle 2 onto end of needle 1—12 sts each on 2 needles. Cut yarn, leaving a 15" (38-cm) tail. Thread tail on a tapestry needle and use the Kitchener st (Glossary, page 117) to graft sts tog. Weave in loose ends. Block on sock blockers or under a damp towel.

FLUTED PATTERN
(multiple of 6 sts)

Rnd 1: *K1, p5; rep from *.
Rnd 2: *K2, p4; rep from *.
Rnd 3: *K3, p3; rep from *.
Rnd 4: *K4, p2; rep from *.
Rnd 5: *K5, p1; rep from *.
Repeat Rnds 1–5 for pattern.

Pneumatic tire invented	Singer produces electric sewing machine	Eiffel Tower completed	Hermine Cadolle creates the first bra	Britain has 27,811 km of railroad	London Tube opens	Tchaikovsky's *Sleeping Beauty* ballet first performed	Ellis Island opened	Thermos flask invented	Marie Corelli writes *Lillith*	Zipper invented in U.S.	First escalator built
1888	1889			1890			1892			1893	1894

Gentleman's Sock
in Railway Stitch

Weldon's, *Volume 4, Tenth Series, 1889, page 7*

Original specifies 4 ounces gray and ½ ounce white hosiery yarn, Peacock quality from Faudel & Phillips; four steel #15 (U.S. 000; 1.5 mm) needles.

This sock is worked in an unconventional way, with the "seam" stitch placed 15 stitches after the round begins and the foot worked with what is usually the last needle counted as the first. The first needle holds the stitches for the left side of the heel flap; what we normally designate as the first needle holds the stitches for the right side of the heel. I worked this sock almost as the pattern was written, with a French Heel and Flat Toe, except that I used a larger needle size, worked more rows on the leg and foot than specified (to add needed length), and picked up fewer gusset stitches. The pattern for the leg and the top of the foot is a six-row repeat of knit and purl stitches that creates an interesting woven-looking fabric. The subtle color change in the heel and toe stripes adds even more interest to these man's socks.

SPECIFICATIONS

Finished Size 8" (20.5 cm) foot circumference, 8½" (21.5 cm) long from cast-on edge to top of heel flap, and 10½" (26.5 cm) long from back of heel to tip of toe. To fit men's U.S. shoe sizes 9½ to 10½.

Yarn About 460 yd (421 m) of 1 main color and 230 yd (210 m) of 1 contrasting color of fingering-weight (Super Fine #1) yarn. We used Skacel Fortissima/ Socka (75% wool, 25% nylon; 230 yd [210 m]/50 g; 20 wraps per inch): #1058 gray (MC), 2 skeins, and #2414 tan (CC), 1 skein. *Note:* You'll need 3 skeins of MC if you lengthen the leg or foot.

Needles Size 0 (2 mm): set of 4 double-pointed. Adjust needle size if necessary to obtain the correct gauge.

Notions Stitch marker (m); tapestry needle.

Gauge 15 sts and 22 rnds = 2" (5 cm) in St st worked in the rnd, before blocking.

> **RAILWAY STITCH** (multiple of 5 sts)
> *Rnds 1 and 2:* *K1, p1, k1, p2; rep from *.
> *Rnd 3:* Knit.
> *Rnds 4 and 5:* *K1, p2, k1, p1; rep from *.
> *Rnd 6:* Knit.
> Repeat Rnds 1–6 for pattern.

LEG

With MC, CO 81 sts onto 1 needle. Divide sts onto 3 needles so that there are 30 sts on needle 1, 25 sts on needle 2, and 26 sts on needle 3. Join for working in the rnd, being careful not to twist sts, and place marker (pm) after first st to denote beg of rnd.

Cuff: Work k2, p1 ribbing for 24 rnds —piece should measure 2¼" (5.5 cm) from beg. *Next rnd:* Knit to last 2 sts, k2tog—80 sts rem.

Leg: Place another marker before 16th st of the rnd—this is the "seam" st and will be knitted every rnd unless otherwise specified.

Rnds 1–11: Work 11 rnds railway st patt (see above), ending with Rnd 5 of patt.

Rnd 12: (Rnd 6 of patt) Knit to 3 sts before seam st m, k2tog, k1, slip marker (sl m), k2 (seam st is the first of these 2 sts), sl 1, k1, psso, work to end of rnd as established—78 sts; seam st is now 15th st of rnd.

Rnds 13 and 14: (Rnds 1 and 2 of patt) [K1, p1, k1, p2] 2 times, k2, p2, sl m, k1 (seam st), p2, k1, *k1, p1, k1, p2; rep from * to end.

Rnd 15: (Rnd 3 of patt) Knit.

Rnds 16 and 17: (Rnds 4 and 5 of patt) [K1, p2, k1, p1] 2 times, [k1, p1] 2 times, sl m, [k1, p1] 2 times (seam st is first k1), *k1, p2, k1, p1; rep from * to end.

Rnd 18: (Rnd 6 of patt) Knit to 3 sts before seam st m, k2tog, k1, sl m, k2 (seam st is the first of these 2 sts), sl 1, k1, psso, knit to end—76 sts; seam st is now 14th st of rnd.

Rnds 19 and 20: (Rnds 1 and 2 of patt) [K1, p1, k1, p2] 2 times, k1, p2, sl m, k1, p2, *k1, p1, k1, p2; rep from * to end.

Rnd 21: (Rnd 3 of patt) Knit.

Rnds 22 and 23: (Rnds 4 and 5 of patt) [K1, p2, k1, p1] 2 times, k2, p1, sl m, k1 (seam st), p1, k1, *k1, p2, k1, p1; rep from * to end.

Rnd 24: (Rnd 6 of patt) Knit to 2 sts before seam st m, k2tog, sl m, k1 (seam st), sl 1, k1, psso, knit to end—74 sts; seam st is now 13th st of rnd.

Rnds 25 and 26: (Rnds 1 and 2 of patt) [K1, p1, k1, p2] 2 times, k1, p1, sl m, k1 (seam st), p1, *k1, p1, k1, p2; rep from * to end.

Rnd 27: (Rnd 3 of patt) Knit to 2 sts before seam st m, sl 1, k1, psso, sl m, k1 (seam st), k2tog, knit to end—72 sts; seam st is now 12th st of rnd.

Rnds 28 and 29: (Rnds 4 and 5 of patt) [K1, p2, k1, p1] 2 times, k1, sl m, p1 (seam st), *k1, p2, k1, p1; rep from * to end.

Rnd 30: (Rnd 6 of patt) Knit to 1 st before m, sl 1, remove marker, k2tog, psso, knit to end—70 sts; 20 sts on needle 1, 25 sts each on needles 2 and 3.

Rnds 31–69: Rep 6-rnd railway st patt 6 more times, then work Rnds 1–3 once more—11½ patt reps have been completed; piece measures about 8½" (21.5 cm) from beg.

HEEL

Heel flap: K10, p1 (seam st), k18, turn. Sl 1, p36—37 heel sts on 1 needle. Hold rem 33 sts on 2 needles to be worked later for instep. Work heel sts back and forth in rows as foll:

Row 1: (RS) Sl 1, k17, p1, k18.

Row 2: (WS) Sl 1, p36.

Rep Rows 1 and 2 once more. Change to CC and work Rows 1 and 2 once. Change to MC and work Rows 1 and 2 once. Rep the last 4 rows 5 more times, alternating colors every 2 rows, then work 2 more rows with CC—30 rows total worked; 15 chain sts (slipped selvedge sts) along each edge of heel flap. Cut off MC.

Safety pin invented	Domestic sewing machine patented	Queen Victoria administered chloroform	Typewriter patented	Charles Dickens publishes *A Tale of Two Cities*	Commercial baby food launched in Germany	Saccharine discovered	Indigo synthesized in Germany	Male farm laborers and domestics able to vote	First motor cars	26,000 homes in U.K. have a telephone	Eastman Kodak camera available in U.S.
1849	1851	1853	1854	1859	1867	1879	1880	1884	1885	1887	1888

Turn heel: With CC, work short rows as foll:

Row 1: (RS) Sl 1, k17, p1, k1, sl 1, k1, psso, k1, turn.

Row 2: (WS) Sl 1, p4, p2tog, p1, turn.

For remainder of heel turning, work sts in St st, except for center seam st, which is purled on both RS and WS rows as established.

Row 3: Sl 1, work to 1 st before gap made on previous row, sl 1, k1, psso, k1, turn.

Row 4: Sl 1, work to 1 st before gap made on previous row, p2tog, p1, turn.

Rep Rows 3 and 4 until all heel sts have been worked, ending with Row 4—21 sts rem. Cut off CC.

Gussets: *Note:* The gusset sts are set up differently from the usual arrangement: The rnd begs at the beg of the heel sts (not the center of the heel). Join MC with RS facing to the left side of the instep sts, at the base of the heel flap, ready to pick up sts along left edge of flap, beginning after instep sts and working towards heel turn.

Rnd 1: With needle 1, pick up and knit 17 sts along left side of heel flap, then knit across first 11 heel sts; with needle 2, knit 10 rem heel sts, pick up and knit 17 sts along right side of heel flap; with needle 3, k1, work railway st beg with Rnd 4 over next 30 instep sts, k2—88 sts; 28 sts on needle 1, 27 sts on needle 2, 33 instep sts on needle 3. Rnd begins at end of instep sts.

Rnd 2: Work even, maintaining established patt on instep sts.

Rnd 3: On needle 1, k1, sl 1, k1, psso, knit to end; on needle 2, knit to last 3 sts, k2tog, k1; on needle 3, work in established patt— 2 sts dec'd.

Rnd 4: Work even as established.

Rep Rnds 3 and 4 ten more times—66 sts rem; 17 sts on needle 1, 16 sts on needle 2, 33 instep sts on needle 3.

FOOT

Cont even in patt until 11½ patt reps (69 rnds) have been worked from the gusset pick-up rnd, ending with Rnd 6 of railway st patt; foot measures 8" (20.5 cm) from back of heel, or 2½" (6.5 cm) less than desired total length. With MC, knit 2 rnds. With CC, knit 2 rnds.

TOE

Change to MC.

Rnd 1: On needle 1, k1, sl 1, k1, psso, knit to end; on needle 2, knit to last 3 sts, k2tog, k1; on needle 3, k1, sl 1, k1, psso, knit to last 3 sts, k2tog, k1—4 sts dec'd.

Rnd 2: Knit.

Change to CC and rep Rnds 1 and 2—58 sts rem. Rep Rnds 1 and 2, alternating 2 rnds each of MC and CC, 5 more times, ending with a CC stripe—38 sts rem; 10 sts on needle 1, 9 sts on needle 2, 19 sts on needle 3. Cut MC, and rep Rnds 1 and 2 with CC 4 more times—22 sts rem; 6 sts on needle 1, 5 sts on needle 2, 11 sts on needle 3. The original pattern says "arrange the remaining sts on one needle and cast off, sewing the cast off sts together to close the hole." I recommend placing the sts on needles 1 and 2 onto the same needle so that there are 11 sts each on 2 needles. Cut yarn, leaving a 12" (30.5-cm) tail. Thread tail on a tapestry needle, and use the Kitchener st (Glossary, page 117) to graft sts tog. Weave in loose ends. Block on sock blockers or under a damp towel.

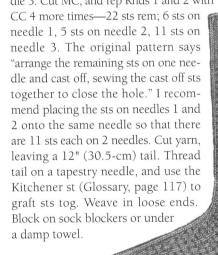

Pneumatic tire invented	Singer produces electric sewing machine	Eiffel Tower completed	Hermine Cadolle creates the first bra	Britain has 27,811 km of railroad	London Tube opens	Tchaikovsky's *Sleeping Beauty* ballet first performed	Ellis Island opened	Thermos flask invented	Marie Corelli writes *Lillith*	Zipper invented in U.S.	First escalator built
1888	1889		1890			1892				1893	1894

GENTLEMAN'S SOCK

with Lozenge Pattern

Weldon's, *Volume 10, Twenty-eighth Series, 1895, page 13*

Original specifies 4½ ounces of Baldwin's 4-ply fingering wool made by Messrs. John Paton, Son & Co., Alloa; four steel #15 (U.S. 000; 1.5 mm) needles.

The introduction for this sock design in *Weldon's* calls the pattern a "complete change from the usual plain-knitted article." The original leg measured 12" (30.5 cm) long, and the foot measured 10" (25.5 cm) long. It is a large sock, perfect for a man with a U.S. shoe size 11 or larger. To make a smaller size, you need to use smaller needles or reduce the number of stitches in the pattern. This sock has a Round Heel and Wide Toe.

SPECIFICATIONS

Finished Size 9" (23 cm) foot circumference, 10½" (26.5 cm) long from cast-on edge to top of heel flap, and 11" (28 cm) long from back of heel to tip of toe. To fit men's U.S. shoe sizes 11 to 12.

Yarn About 600 yd (549 m) of fingering-weight (Super Fine #1) yarn. We used Sunbeam St. Ives (80% wool, 20% nylon; 200 yd [182 m]/50 g; 19 wraps per inch): #3104 grouse, 3 skeins.

Needles Size 0 (2 mm): set of 4 double-pointed. Adjust needle size if necessary to obtain the correct gauge.

Notions Stitch marker (m); tapestry needle.

Gauge 17 sts and 24 rnds = 2" (5 cm) in St st worked in the rnd, before blocking.

LEG

CO 78 sts onto 1 needle. Divide sts onto 3 needles so that there are 30 sts on needle 1, and 24 sts each on needles 2 and 3. Join for working in the rnd, being careful not to twist sts, and place marker (pm) after first st to denote beg of rnd.

Cuff: Work k3, p3 ribbing for 9 rnds. Purl 1 rnd. Rep the last 10 rnds 2 more times, then work 9 rnds of k3, p3 ribbing once more.

Next rnd: Purl, inc 1 st each on needles 2 and 3, and at the end of the rnd redistribute sts by purling the first 2 sts from needle 1 onto the end of needle 3—80 sts; 28 sts on needle 1, 25 sts on needle 2, and 27 sts on needle 3. Reposition marker at end of last rnd—piece should measure about 3½" (9 cm) from beg.

Leg: Work lozenge patt as foll:

Rnd 1: *K9, p1; rep from * (the last purl st of each rnd is the "seam" st and is always purled).

Rnd 2: *P1, k7, p1, k1; rep from * to last 10 sts, p1, k7, p2.

Rnd 3: K1, *p1, k5, p1, k3; rep from * to last 9 sts, p1, k5, p1, k1, p1.

Rnd 4: K2, *p1, k3, p1, k5; rep from * to last 8 sts, p1, k3, p1, k2, p1.

Rnd 5: K3, *p1, k1, p1, k7; rep from * to last 7 sts, p1, k1, p1, k3, p1.

Rnd 6: K4, *p1, k9; rep from * to last 6 sts, p1, k4, p1.

Rnd 7: K3, *p1, k1, p1, k7; rep from * to last 7 sts, p1, k1, p1, k3, p1.

Rnd 8: K2, *p1, k3, p1, k5; rep from * to last 8 sts, p1, k3, p1, k2, p1.

Rnd 9: K1, *p1, k5, p1, k3; rep from * to last 9 sts, p1, k5, p1, k1, p1.

Rnd 10: *P1, k7, p1, k1; rep from * to last 10 sts, p1, k7, p2.

Rep Rnds 1–10 seven more times, then work Rnds 1–6 once more—piece should measure about 10½" (26.5 cm) from beg.

HEEL

Heel flap: K20, sl rem sts from needle 1 onto needle 2, turn—33 sts on needle 2.

Row 1: (WS) Sl 1, p19, k1 (seam st), p20, sl rem sts from needle 3 onto needle 2, turn—41 heel sts on one needle. Redistribute rem 39 sts on 2 needles to be worked later for instep. Work 41 heel sts back and forth in rows as foll:

Row 2: (RS) Sl 1, k19, p1, k20.

Row 3: (WS) Sl 1, p19, k1, p20.

Rep Rows 2 and 3 until a total of 30 heel rows have been worked, ending with Row 3; 15 chain sts (slipped selvedge sts) along each edge of heel flap.

Turn heel: Work short rows as foll:

Row 1: (RS) K22, sl 1, k1, psso, k1, turn.

Row 2: (WS) Sl 1, p4, p2tog, p1, turn.

Row 3: Sl 1, knit to 1 st before gap made on previous row, sl 1, k1, psso, k1, turn.

Row 4: Sl 1, purl to 1 st before gap made on previous row, p2tog, p1, turn.

Rep Rows 3 and 4 until all sts have been worked—23 heel sts rem.

Gussets: Rejoin for working in the rnd as foll:

Rnd 1: With needle 1, k23 heel sts, then pick up and knit 17 sts along right side of heel flap; with needle 2, work 39 instep sts in established lozenge patt; with needle 3, pick up and knit 17 sts along left side of heel flap, then knit the first 12 sts from needle 1 again—96 sts total; 28 sts on needle 1, 39 instep sts on needle 2, 29 sts on needle 3. Rnd begins at back of heel.

Rnd 2: On needle 1, knit to last st, p1; on needle 2, work instep sts in established patt; on needle 3, p1, knit to end.

Rnd 3: On needle 1, knit to last 3 sts, k2tog, p1; on needle 2, work instep sts in established patt; on needle 3, p1, sl 1, k1, psso, knit to end—2 sts dec'd.

Rep Rnds 2 and 3 eight more times—78 sts

Hershey chocolate bar introduced in the U.S.	A.C. Doyle publishes *Adventures of Sherlock Holmes*	X-rays developed in Germany	First kiss on the silver screen	Ice cream cone invented	Lifebuoy soap launched by W. Lever Co.	Aspirin invented by F. Bayer and Co.	First hand-held electric hair dryer	Johann Vaaler patents paper clips	First driving school in England	Upright electric vacuum cleaner	Gas-powered lawn mower
1894	1895	1896		1897	1899		1900	1901		1902	

rem; 19 sts on needle 1, 39 instep sts on needle 2, 20 sts on needle 3.

FOOT

Cont even as established until 74 rnds have been worked from gusset pick-up rnd, 160 total rnds of lozenge patt for leg and foot—foot should measure about 8¾" (22 cm) from back of heel, or about 2¼" (5.5 cm) less than desired total length.

TOE

Rnd 1: On needle 1, knit to last 4 sts, k2tog, k2; on needle 2, k2, sl 1, k1, psso, knit to last 4 sts, k2tog, k2; on needle 3, k2, sl 1, k1, psso, knit to end—4 sts dec'd.
Rnd 2: Knit.

Rep Rnds 1 and 2 twelve more times—26 sts rem; 6 sts on needle 1, 13 instep sts on needle 2, 7 sts on needle 3. Knit sts from needle 1 onto needle 3—13 sts each on 2 needles. Cut yarn, leaving a 15" (38-cm) tail. Thread tail on a tapestry needle and use the Kitchener st (Glossary, page 117) to graft sts tog. Weave in loose ends. Block on sock blockers or under a damp towel.

First automatic tea maker	Thomas Sullivan invents the tea bag	Electric washing machine launched in the U.S.	Rowenta launches electric iron	Bleriot flies across the English Channel	Neon lighting invented	Coco Chanel launches women's sportswear	Wristwatch becomes popular for men	Deep-freeze invented	In Britain, men over 21 and women over 30 with property allowed to vote	Universal adult suffrage in the U.K. adds women 21 to 30 and abolishes property qualification
1902	1904	1907	1908	1909	1910	1913	1914	1917	1918	1928

BED SOCK

in Lemon Pattern Fancy Knit Stripe

Weldon's, *Volume 11, Thirteenth Series, 1896, page 8*

Original specifies 2½ ounces of unshrinkable vest wool (pink); four steel #14 (U.S. 00; 1.75 mm) and #12 (U.S. size 2; 2.75 mm) needles.

These soft and cozy bed socks seem like the perfect example of Victorian luxury. The pattern is an allover openwork rib, even on the bottom of the foot, that yields a very stretchy and comfortable pair of sleeping socks. I have followed the original pattern through the Dutch Heel vari-ation, but I've changed the toe ending from a simple bound-off and sewn toe seam to a grafted tip. The original design also calls for an optional crochet edging at the top, which I have omitted. To main-tain maximum stretch, I have not blocked these socks.

45

SPECIFICATIONS

Finished Size 8" (20.5 cm) foot circumference, 7" (18 cm) long from cast-on edge to top of heel flap, and 9" (23 cm) long from back of heel to tip of toe. To fit women's U.S. shoe sizes 6½ to 7½, but can stretch larger.

Yarn About 285 yd (261 m) of fingering-weight (Super Fine #1) yarn. We used Mountain Colors Cashmere (100% cashmere; 95 yd [87 m]/1 oz; 19 wraps per inch): ladyslipper, 3 skeins.

Note: You'll need 4 skeins if you lengthen the leg or foot.

Needles Size 2 (2.75 mm): set of 4 or 5 double-pointed. Adjust needle size if necessary to obtain the correct gauge.

Notions Stitch marker (m); tapestry needle.

Gauge 22 sts and 19½ rnds = 2" (5 cm) in openwork ribbing worked in the rnd, unstretched.

LEG

CO 78 sts onto 1 needle. Divide sts on 3 needles so that 30 sts are on needle 1, 24 sts are on needle 2, and 24 sts are on needle 3. Join for working in the rnd, being careful not to twist sts, and place marker (pm) after first st to denote beg of rnd. Cont as foll:

Rnds 1–3: *K3, p3; rep from *.

Rnd 4: *Yo, k3tog, yo, p3; rep from *.

Rnds 5–20: Rep Rnds 1–4 four more times.

Rnd 21: [K3, p3] 8 times, k3, p2tog, p1, k3, p1, p2tog, [k3, p3] 3 times—76 sts rem.

Rnd 22: [K3, p3] 8 times, k3, p2, sl 1, k2tog, psso, p2, [k3, p3] 3 times—74 sts rem.

Rnd 23: [K3, p3] 8 times, k3, p2tog, p1, p2tog, [k3, p3] 3 times—72 sts rem; one complete patt rep has been eliminated from the center back leg.

Rnd 24: *Yo, k3tog, yo, p3; rep from *.

Rnds 25–68: Rep Rnds 1–4 eleven more times, ending with Rnd 4—68 rnds have been worked; if counted straight up along a single column of eyelet holes, there will be 17 holes; piece measures about 7" (18 cm) from beg.

HEEL

Hold first 33 sts of rnd on 2 needles to be worked later for instep. Turn work in preparation for working heel on last 39 sts of rnd, and work heel sts back and forth in rows as foll:

Heel flap:

Row 1: (WS) Sl 1, k2, [p3, k3] 6 times, turn.

Row 2: (RS) Sl 1, p2, [k3, p3] 6 times, turn.

Row 3: Sl 1, k2, [p3, k3] 6 times, turn.

Row 4: Sl 1, p2, [yo, k3tog, yo, p3] 6 times, turn.

Rep Rows 1–4 until a total of 24 rows have been worked. *Next row:* (WS) P12, [k3, p3] 2 times, k3, p12.

Turn heel: Cont in short rows as foll:

Row 1: (RS) K12, [p3, k3] 2 times, p3, sl 1, k1, psso, turn.

Row 2: (WS) Sl 1, [k3, p3] 2 times, k3, p2tog, turn.

Row 3: Sl 1, [p3, k3] 2 times, p3, sl 1, k1, psso, turn.

Row 4: Sl 1, [k3, p3] 2 times, k3, p2tog, turn.

Rep Rows 3 and 4 until all sts have been worked, ending with Rnd 4—17 heel sts rem.

Gussets: Rejoin for working in the rnd as foll:

Rnd 1: With needle 1, work across heel sts as foll: sl 1, [p3, k3] 2 times, p3, k1, then pick up and knit 17 sts along right side of heel flap; with needle 2, work across first 30 instep sts in patt as established; with needle 3, k3 rem instep sts, pick up and knit 17 sts along left side of heel flap, and work the first 10 sts from needle 1 again as foll: k1, p3, k3, p3—84 sts total; 24 sts on needle 1, 30 sts each on needles 2 and 3. Rnd begins at back of heel.

Rnds 2, 3, 5, 6, and 7: *K3, p3; rep from *.

Rnd 4: *Yo, k3tog, yo, p3, rep from *.

Rnd 8: On needle 1, [yo, k3tog, yo, p3] 2 times, yo, k3tog, yo, p1, p2tog, yo, k3tog, yo, p2tog, p1; on needle 2, [yo, k3tog, yo, p3] 5 times; on needle 3, yo, k3tog, yo, p1, p2tog, yo, k3tog, yo, p2tog, p1, [yo, k3tog, yo, p3] 3 times—80 sts rem.

Rnds 9–11: On needle 1, [k3, p3] 2 times, [k3, p2] 2 times; on needle 2, [k3, p3] 5 times; on needle 3, [k3, p2] 2 times, [k3, p3] 3 times.

Rnd 12: On needle 1, [yo, k3tog, yo, p3] 2 times, yo, k3tog, yo, p2, k3tog, p2; on needle 2, [yo, k3tog, yo, p3] 5 times; on needle 3, yo, k3tog, yo, p2, k3tog, p2, [yo, k3tog, yo, p3] 3 times—76 sts rem.

Hershey chocolate bar introduced in the U.S.	A.C. Doyle publishes *Adventures of Sherlock Holmes*	X-rays developed in Germany	First kiss on the silver screen	Ice cream cone invented	Lifebuoy soap launched by W. Lever Co.	Aspirin invented by F. Bayer and Co.	First hand-held electric hair dryer	Johann Vaaler patents paper clips	First driving school in England	Upright electric vacuum cleaner	Gas-powered lawn mower
1894		1895	1896		1897	1899		1900	1901		1902

Rnds 13–15: On needle 1, [k3, p3] 2 times, k3, p5; on needle 2, [k3, p3] 5 times; on needle 3, k3, p5, [k3, p3] 3 times.

Rnd 16: On needle 1, [yo, k3tog, yo, p3] 2 times, yo, k3tog, yo, p1, p3tog, p1; on needle 2, [yo, k3tog, yo, p3] 5 times; on needle 3, yo, k3tog, yo, p1, p3tog, p1, [yo, k3tog, yo, p3] 3 times—72 sts rem.

Rnds 17–19: *K3, p3; rep from *.

Rnd 20: *Yo, k3tog, yo, p3; rep from *.

Rep Rnds 17–20 eight more times—52 rnds completed from gusset pick-up rnd; if counted straight up along a single column of eyelet holes, there will be 13 holes from gusset pick-up rnd. Piece should measure about 7½" (19 cm) from back of heel, or 1½" (3.8 cm) less than desired total length.

TOE

Rnds 1–3: *K3, p3; rep from *.

Rnd 4: [K3, p3, k3, p3tog] 2 times, [k3, p3] 3 times, k3, p3tog, k3, p3, k3, p3tog, [k3, p3] 2 times—64 sts rem.

Rnds 5–7: Work all sts as they appear, working p1 at each p3tog of the previous rnd.

Rnd 8: K3, p3, [k2, k3tog, k2, p3] 2 times, [k3, p3] 2 times, [k2, k3tog, k2, p3] 2 times, k3, p3—56 sts rem.

Rnds 9–11: Work all sts as they appear, working k1 at each k3tog of previous rnd.

Rnd 12: K3, [p3, k1, k3tog, k1] 2 times, [p3, k3] 2 times, [p3, k1, k3tog, k1] 2 times, p3, k3, p3—48 sts rem.

Rnds 13 and 14: *K3, p3; rep from *.

Rnd 15: K2tog, k1, p2tog, p1, k2tog, k1, p3tog, [k2tog, k1, p2tog, p1] 3 times, k2tog, k1, p3tog, [k2tog, k1, p2tog, p1] 2 times—30 sts rem.

Arrange sts so that 15 instep sts are on one needle and 15 sole sts for bottom of foot are on another needle. With yarn threaded on a tapestry needle and using the Kitchener st (Glossary, page 117), graft sts tog. Weave in loose ends. Block on sock blockers or under a damp towel.

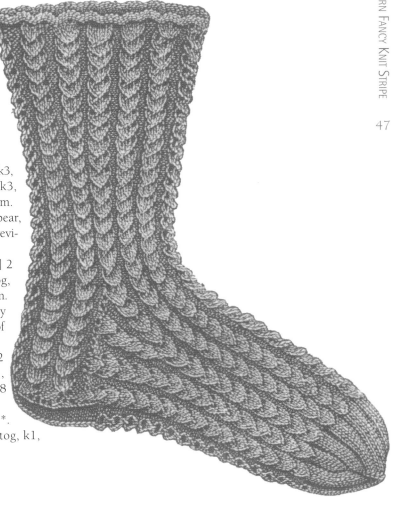

First automatic tea maker	Thomas Sullivan invents the tea bag	Electric washing machine launched in the U.S.	Rowenta launches electric iron	Bleriot flies across the English Channel	Neon lighting invented	Coco Chanel launches women's sportswear	Wristwatch becomes popular for men	Deep-freeze invented	In Britain, men over 21 and women over 30 with property allowed to vote	Universal adult suffrage in the U.K. adds women 21 to 30 and abolishes property qualification
1902	1904	1907	1908	1909	1910	1913	1914	1917	1918	1928

CYCLING OR GOLF STOCKINGS

with Fancy Cuff in Trellis Pattern

Weldon's, *Volume 12, Sixth Series,*
1897, pages 5 and 10

Original specifies 4 ounces of 4-ply fingering yarn;
four steel #15 (U.S. 000; 1.5 mm) needles.

This stocking is adapted from several patterns in *Weldon's Practical Stocking Knitter*, Volume 12, Sixth Series. This series contains designs for cycling and golf stockings, all sized for men or boys. I have used one of the many cuff patterns offered, and applied it to a boy's ribbed stocking. Although the original cuff pattern calls for two colors, I have used three, and have worked the stocking leg in a size to fit a woman. I've used a Welsh heel and a Star Toe of Three Points for this fun-to-knit stocking.

SPECIFICATIONS

Finished Size 7" (18 cm) foot circumference, 13" (33 cm) long from cuff turning round to top of heel flap, and 9½" (24 cm) long from back of heel to tip of toe. To fit women's U.S. shoe sizes 8 to 9.

Yarn About 525 yd (480 m) of 1 main color and 175 yd (160 m) each of 2 contrasting colors of fingering-weight (Super Fine #1) yarn. **We used** Wooly West Footpath (85% wool, 15% nylon; 175 yd [160 m] 2 oz; 18 wraps per inch): lichen (MC), 3 skeins; yarrow (CC1) and grape (CC2), 1 skein each.

Needles Size 1 (2.5 mm): set of 4 double-pointed. Adjust needle size if necessary to obtain the correct gauge.

Notions Stitch marker (m); tapestry needle.

Gauge 15 sts and 20 rnds = 2" (5 cm) in St st worked in the rnd, before blocking.

LEG

With MC, CO 80 sts onto 1 needle. Divide sts as evenly as possible on 3 needles. Join for working in the rnd, being careful not to twist sts, and place marker (pm) after first st to denote beg of rnd.

Cuff: Work k2, p2 ribbing for 4 rnds. Change to CC2 and knit 1 rnd, then purl 1 rnd. Change to CC1 and knit 1 rnd, then purl 1 rnd. Cut off CC1. With MC and CC2, work Rnds 1–23 of Trellis chart (page 51) in St st. When chart is complete, join CC1 and knit 1 rnd, then purl 1 rnd. Cut off CC1. Change to CC2 and knit 1 rnd, then purl 1 rnd. Cut off CC2. With MC, work 2 rnds in k2, p2 ribbing. Purl 3 rnds. *Next rnd:* *P18, p2tog; rep from *—76 sts rem; cuff measures about 3¾" (9.5 cm) from beg. Turn the work inside out so WS of cuff is facing you. The last needle of the previous rnd will be the first needle you work in this new arrangement, and turning the work inside out in this manner will leave a small hole in the sock where you reversed direction, which you can darn closed when the sock is finished. This will place the RS of the cuff patt on the public side of the stocking when the cuff is turned down. Work k2, p2 ribbing for 25 rnds—piece should measure about 2½" (6.5 cm) from cuff turning rnd.

Leg: Change to k3, p1 ribbing and work a total of 24 rnds—piece should measure about 5" (12.5 cm) from cuff turning rnd. *Dec rnd:* K1, sl 1, k1, psso, work in established rib to last 4 sts of rnd, k2tog, k1, p1— 2 sts dec'd. Work 7 rnds as established. Rep

the last 8 rnds 6 more times, then work dec rnd once more—60 sts rem. Cont in rib patt until leg measures 13" (33 cm) from cuff turning rnd.

HEEL

Heel flap: Knit the first 15 sts of rnd, turn, and work 31 sts onto one needle for heel flap as foll: (WS) Sl 1, p14, k1 ("seam st"), p15. Place the rem 29 sts on 2 needles to be worked later for instep (first and last sts of instep should be purl sts). Work 31 heel flap sts back and forth in rows as foll:

Row 1: (RS) Sl 1, k14, p1 ("seam st"), k15, turn.

Row 2: (WS) Sl 1, p14, k1, p15, turn.

Rep Rows 1 and 2 fifteen times total—30 heel flap rows have been worked; 15 chain sts (slipped selvedge sts) along each edge of heel flap.

Turn heel: Work short rows as foll:

Row 1: (RS) *Sl 1, k4, yo, k2tog, k5, k2tog, k1, p1 (seam st), k1, k2tog, k5, k2tog, turn.

Row 2: (WS) Yo, purl to seam st, k1 (seam st), purl to 10 sts beyond seam st (purling yo of previous row, and counting it as 1 purl st), turn.

Row 3: Yo, k2tog, k5, k2tog, k1, p1 (seam st), k1, k2tog, k5, k2tog (yo of previous row and next st), turn.

Rep Rows 2 and 3 four more times; decs on either side of seam st will not be symmetrical mirror images of each other—18 sts rem (including yos).

Row 4: (WS) Sl 1, purl to seam st, k1 (seam st), purl to last 2 sts, p2tog—17 sts; 8 sts on either side of seam st.

Gussets: Rejoin for working in the rnd as foll:

Rnd 1: With RS facing and needle 1, knit across 17 heel sts, pick up and knit 15 sts along right side of heel flap; with needle 2,

Hershey chocolate bar introduced in the U.S.	A.C. Doyle publishes *Adventures of Sherlock Holmes*	X-rays developed in Germany	First kiss on the silver screen	Ice cream cone invented	Lifebuoy soap launched by W. Lever Co.	Aspirin invented by F. Bayer and Co.	First hand-held electric hair dryer	Johann Vaaler patents paper clips	First driving school in England	Upright electric vacuum cleaner	Gas-powered lawn mower
1894		1895	1896		1897	1899		1900	1901		1902

work across 29 instep sts in established rib patt; with needle 3, pick up and knit 15 sts along left side of heel flap, then knit the first 9 sts from needle 1 again—76 sts total; 23 sts on needle 1, 29 instep sts on needle 2, 24 sts on needle 3. Rnd begins at center of heel.

Rnd 2: On needle 1, knit to last 3 sts, k2tog, k1; on needle 2, work sts as they appear (knit the knits and purl the purls); on needle 3, k1, sl 1, k1, psso, knit to end—74 sts; 22 sts on needle 1, 29 instep sts on needle 2, 23 sts on needle 3.

Rnd 3: Work even as established.

Rnd 4: On needle 1, knit to last 3 sts, k2tog, k1; on needle 2, work even in patt; on needle 3, k1, sl 1, k1, psso, knit to end—2 sts dec'd.

Rep Rnds 3 and 4 six more times—60 sts rem; 16 sts on needle 1, 15 sts on needle 2, and 29 instep sts on needle 3.

FOOT

Work as established until foot measures 6½" (16.5 cm) from back of heel, or 3" (7.5 cm) less than desired total length.

TOE

Arrange sts so that there are 20 sts on each needle by slipping the first 5 instep sts to needle 1, and the last 4 instep sts to needle 3.

Rnd 1: *K19, p1; rep from *.

Rnds 2–5: Knit.

Rnd 6: *P2tog, k15, p2tog, k1; rep from *—54 sts rem.

Rnds 7–10: Knit.

Rnd 11: *K1, p2tog, k11, p2tog, k2; rep from *—48 sts rem.

Rnds 12–15: Knit.

Rnd 16: *K2, p2tog, k7, p2tog, k3; rep from *—42 sts rem.

Trellis

▨	grape CC2
+	lichen MC
☐	pattern repeat

Rnds 17–20: Knit.

Rnd 21: *K3, p2tog, k3, p2tog, k4; rep from *—36 sts rem.

Rnds 22–25: Knit.

Rnd 26: *K4, p3tog, k5; rep from *—30 sts rem.

Rnd 27: *K3, p3tog, k4; rep from *—24 sts rem.

Rnd 28: *K2, p3tog, k3; rep from *—18 sts rem.

Rnd 29: *K1, p3tog, k2; rep from *—12 sts rem.

Rnd 30: *P3tog, k1; rep from *—6 sts rem. Cut yarn. Thread tail on a tapestry needle, draw through rem sts, and pull up snugly to close end of toe. Weave in loose ends. Block on sock blockers or under a damp towel.

First automatic tea maker	Thomas Sullivan invents the tea bag	Electric washing machine launched in the U.S.	Rowenta launches electric iron	Bleriot flies across the English Channel	Neon lighting invented	Coco Chanel launches women's sportswear	Wristwatch becomes popular for men	Deep-freeze invented	In Britain, men over 21 and women over 30 with property allowed to vote	Universal adult suffrage in the U.K. adds women 21 to 30 and abolishes property qualification
1902	1904	1907	1908	1909	1910	1913	1914	1917	1918	1928

HEELLESS
SLEEPING SOCKS

Weldon's, *Volume 12, Thirty-fifth Series, 1897, page 9*

Original specifies Patons petticoat fleecy in white or scarlet; four #10 (U.S. 3; 3 mm) needles.

The original pattern calls for "rather thicker pins than are generally employed" to give more elasticity. The text also notes that these socks are easy to make and "as the foot makes a fresh place for itself" every time they are worn, they are "particularly durable." I've made this sock per the original through the Round Toe, but I've used smaller needles and worked 7½ repeats of the 16-row pattern down the leg, rather than 9. If you want to knit more rounds, you may need more yarn.

SPECIFICATIONS

Finished Size 6½" (16.5 cm) foot circumference, 18" (45.5 cm) long from cast-on edge to tip of toe. To fit women's U.S. shoe sizes 6 to 10.

Yarn About 350 yd (320 m) of fingering-weight (Super Fine #1) yarn. **We used** Mountain Colors Weaver's Wool Quarters (100% wool; 350 yd [320 m]/100 g; 17 wraps per inch): sagebrush, 1 skein.

Needles Size 2 (2.75 mm): set of 4 double-pointed. Adjust needle size if necessary to obtain the correct gauge.

Notions Stitch marker (m); tapestry needle.

Gauge 13 sts and 22 rnds = 2" (5 cm) in St st worked in the rnd, before blocking; 15 sts and 18 rnds = 2" (5 cm) in leg pattern, before blocking.

LEG

CO 48 sts onto 1 needle. Divide sts evenly onto 3 needles (16 sts each needle). Join for working in the rnd, being careful not to twist sts, and place marker (pm) after first st to denote beg of rnd.

Cuff: Work k2, p2 ribbing for 20 rnds—piece should measure 2" (5 cm) from beg.

Leg: Cont in patt as foll:

Rnds 1–4: *P3, k1; rep from *.

Rnds 5–8: *K1, p3; rep from *.

Rnds 9–12: P1, *k1, p3; rep from * to last 3 sts, end k1, p2.

Rnds 13–16: P2, *k1, p3; rep from * to last 2 sts, end k1, p1.

Rep these 16 rnds 6 more times, then work Rnds 1–8 once more—piece should measure about 15½" (39.5 cm) from beg.

TOE

Rnd 1: *K6, k2tog; rep from *—42 sts rem.

Rnds 2–7: Knit.

Rnd 8: *K5, k2tog; rep from *—36 sts rem.

Rnds 9–13: Knit.

Rnd 14: *K4, k2tog; rep from *—30 sts rem.

Rnds 15–18: Knit.

Rnd 19: *K3, k2tog; rep from *—24 sts rem.

Rnds 20–22: Knit.

Rnd 23: *K2, k2tog; rep from *—18 sts rem.

Rnds 24 and 25: Knit.

Rnd 26: *K1, k2tog; rep from *—12 sts rem.

Rnd 27: Knit.

Rnd 28: *K2tog; rep from *—6 sts rem.

Cut yarn, thread tail on a tapestry needle, draw tail through the rem sts, and pull up snugly to close end of toe. Weave in loose ends. Block on sock blockers or under a damp towel.

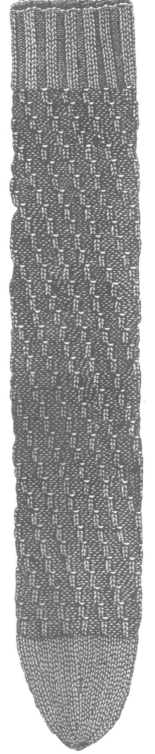

54

Hershey chocolate bar introduced in the U.S.	A.C. Doyle publishes *Adventures of Sherlock Holmes*	X-rays developed in Germany	First kiss on the silver screen	Ice cream cone invented	Lifebuoy soap launched by W. Lever Co.	Aspirin invented by F. Bayer and Co.	First hand-held electric hair dryer	Johann Vaaler patents paper clips	First driving school in England	Upright electric vacuum cleaner	Gas-powered lawn mower
1894		1895	1896		1897	1899		1900	1901		1902

First automatic tea maker	Thomas Sullivan invents the tea bag	Electric washing machine launched in the U.S.	Rowenta launches electric iron	Bleriot flies across the English Channel	Neon lighting invented	Coco Chanel launches women's sportswear	Wristwatch becomes popular for men	Deep-freeze invented	In Britain, men over 21 and women over 30 with property allowed to vote	Universal adult suffrage in the U.K. adds women 21 to 30 and abolishes property qualification
1902	1904	1907	1908	1909	1910	1913	1914	1917	1918	1928

CHILD'S FRENCH SOCK

in Citron Pattern and Diaper Knitting

Weldon's, *Volume 13, Thirty-eighth Series,*
1898, page 6

Original specifies 1 ounce of pure white Shetland
wool; four steel #16 (U.S. 0000; 1.25 mm) needles.

The Child's French Sock was originally designed for a little girl of two or three years. It has a very interesting pattern and seems perfect worked in a larger size for a grown-up. I have stayed faithful to the pattern, except that I've used slipped stitches along the sides of the heel flap. To do so, I've had to pick up a few more stitches than there were slipped stitches available. This sock has a French Heel and a Flat Toe.

Finished Size 7½" (19 cm) foot circumference, 8" (20.5 cm) long from cast-on edge to top of heel flap, and 9½" (24 cm) long from back of heel to tip of toe. To fit women's U.S. shoe sizes 8 to 9.

Yarn About 400 yd (366 m) of fingering-weight (Super Fine #1) yarn. **We used** Jaeger Matchmaker Merino 4 Ply (100% merino; 200 yd [183 m]/50 g; 25 wraps per inch): #0633 strawberry, 2 skeins.

Needles Size 1 (2.5 mm): set of 4 double-pointed. Adjust needle size if necessary to obtain the correct gauge.

Notions Stitch marker (m); tapestry needle.

Gauge 16 sts and 24 rnds = 2" (5 cm) in St st worked in the rnd, before blocking.

Notes

When working lace pattern from chart, take care not to lose any yarnovers that occur at the end of a needle.

When picking up sts along the sides of the heel flap, pick up 18 sts from the 15 chain selvedge sts as foll: *Pick up and knit 1 st from each of the next 3 chain sts by inserting the needle under both halves of each chain st; in the next chain st, pick up and knit 2 sts from the same chain st by inserting the needle under both halves of the chain st and picking up 1 st, then inserting the needle again under the back half of the chain st and picking up 1 st; rep from * 2 more times, pick up and knit 3 sts from each of the last 3 chain sts as before.

LEG

CO 63 sts onto 1 needle. Divide sts evenly on 3 needles (21 sts on each needle). Join for working in the rnd, being careful not to twist sts, and place marker (pm) after first st to denote beg of rnd.

Cuff: *[K2, p2] 2 times, k2, [p1, k1] 5 times, p1; rep from * for each needle. Rep this rnd 19 more times—20 rnds total; piece should measure 1¾" (4.5 cm) from beg.
Leg: *K2, M1 (Glossary, page 115), k6, M1, k2, [p1, k1] 5 times, p1, M1; rep from *— 72 sts. Change to Leg chart (page 59), and rep Rnds 1–6 of chart 11 times—66 chart rnds total; piece should measure about 8" (20.5 cm) from beg.

HEEL

Heel flap:

Row 1: (RS) K12, [p1, k1] 6 times, k12, turn—36 sts on one needle for heel. Hold rem 36 sts on 2 needles to be worked later for instep.

Work 36 heel sts back and forth in rows as foll:

Row 2: (WS) Sl 1, p11, [p1, k1] 6 times, p12.
Row 3: Sl 1, k11, [p1, k1] 6 times, k12.
Rows 4 and 6: Sl 1, p11, [k1, p1] 6 times, p12.
Row 5: Sl 1, k11, [k1, p1] 6 times, k12.
Row 7: Sl 1, k11, [p1, k1] 6 times, k12.
Rep Rows 2–7 (do not rep Row 1) 3 more times, then work Rows 2–6 once more—30 heel rows completed; 15 chain sts (slipped selvedge sts) along each edge of heel flap.
Turn heel: Work short rows as foll:
Row 1: (RS) K19, sl 1, k1, psso, k1, turn.
Row 2: (WS) P4, p2tog, p1, turn.
Row 3: Knit to 1 st before gap made by previous row, sl 1, k1, psso, k1, turn.
Row 4: Purl to 1 st before gap made by previous row, p2tog, p1, turn.
Rep Rows 3 and 4 until all heel sts have been worked—20 heel sts rem.
Gussets: Rejoin for working in the rnd as foll:
Rnd 1: With needle 1, k20 heel sts, then pick up and knit 18 sts along right side of heel flap (see Notes); with needle 2, work 36 instep sts according to Rnd 1 of Foot chart (page 59); with needle 3, pick up and knit 18 sts along left side of heel flap (see Notes), then knit the first 10 sts from needle 1 again—92 sts total; 28 sts each on needles 1 and 3, 36 instep sts on needle 2. Rnd begins at back of heel.
Rnd 2: Knit sts on needles 1 and 3, work instep sts in patt from Foot chart on needle 2.
Rnd 3: On needle 1, knit to last 3 sts, k2tog, k1; on needle 2, work instep sts in patt from Foot chart; on needle 3, k1, sl 1, k1, psso, knit to end—2 sts dec'd.
Rep Rnds 2 and 3 eleven more times—68 sts rem; 16 sts each on needle 1 and 3, 36 instep sts on needle 2.

Hershey chocolate bar introduced in the U.S.	A.C. Doyle publishes *Adventures of Sherlock Holmes*	X-rays developed in Germany	First kiss on the silver screen	Ice cream cone invented	Lifebuoy soap launched by W. Lever Co.	Aspirin invented by F. Bayer and Co.	First hand-held electric hair dryer	Johann Vaaler patents paper clips	First driving school in England	Upright electric vacuum cleaner	Gas-powered lawn mower
1894		1895	1896		1897	1899		1900	1901		1902

Foot

5

3

1

Leg

5

3

1

	knit		sl I, kI, psso
•	purl	o	yo
∕	k2tog		pattern repeat

FOOT

Cont even as established until 10 reps of Foot chart have been completed (21 total patt reps from cuff). *Next rnd:* On needle 1, knit all sts; on needle 2, k2, k2tog, k11, k2tog, k2, sl 1, k1, psso, k11, sl 1, k1, psso, k2; on needle 3, knit to end—64 sts rem; 16 sts each on needles 1 and 3, 32 instep sts on needle 2. Knit all sts for 4 rnds—piece should measure 7¼" (18.5 cm) from back of heel, or 2¼" (5.5 cm) less than desired total length.

TOE

Rnd 1: On needle 1, knit to last 3 sts, k2tog, k1; on needle 2, k1, sl 1, k1, psso, knit to last 3 sts, k2tog, k1; on needle 3, k1, sl 1, k1, psso, knit to end—4 sts dec'd.
Rnd 2: Knit.
Rep Rnds 1 and 2 nine more times—24 sts rem: 6 sts each on needle 1 and 3, 12 instep sts on needle 2. Knit sts from needle 1 onto needle 3—12 sts each on 2 needles. Cut yarn, leaving a 15" (38-cm) tail. Thread tail on a tapestry needle and use the Kitchener st (Glossary, page 117) to graft sts tog. Weave in loose ends. Block on sock blockers or under a damp towel.

CHILD'S FRENCH SOCK

59

First automatic tea maker	Thomas Sullivan invents the tea bag	Electric washing machine launched in the U.S.	Rowenta launches electric iron	Bleriot flies across the English Channel	Neon lighting invented	Coco Chanel launches women's sportswear	Wristwatch becomes popular for men	Deep-freeze invented	In Britain, men over 21 and women over 30 with property allowed to vote	Universal adult suffrage in the U.K. adds women 21 to 30 and abolishes property qualification
1902	1904	1907	1908	1909	1910	1913	1914	1917	1918	1928

CHILD'S FIRST SOCK

in Shell Pattern

Weldon's, *Volume 14, Forty-sixth Series,*
1899, page 1

Original specifies 1 ounce of 2-ply fingering wool manufactured by Messrs. John Paton, Son & Co. Alloa; four #16 (U.S. 0000; 1.25 mm) needles.

This pattern is a larger version of the stocking offered in *Weldon's*. The original was written for a small child. I followed the directions faithfully, working a French Heel and Flat Toe, but I needed to correct a mistake in the heel turn. With size 1 needles and the fingering-weight yarn I chose for the project, the stocking will fit a small woman's foot. The original has six repeats of the shell pattern in the leg section, but I have worked seven repeats. The original is worked with the stitches arranged on three needles, and I have used three needles to carry the stitches, too, with the fourth as the working needle.

61

SPECIFICATIONS

Finished Size 7" (18 cm) foot circumference, 8" (20.5 cm) long from cast-on edge to top of heel flap, and 9" (23 cm) long from back of heel to tip of toe. To fit women's U.S. shoe sizes 6½ to 7½.

Yarn About 370 yd (338 m) of fingering-weight (Super Fine #1) yarn. **We used** Gems Pearl (100% merino, 185 yd [170 m]/50 g; 21 wraps per inch): #47 terra cotta, 2 skeins.

Needles Size 1 (2.5 mm): set of 4 double-pointed. Adjust needle size if necessary to obtain the correct gauge.

Notions Stitch marker (m); tapestry needle.

Gauge 16 sts and 23 rnds = 2" (5 cm) in St st worked in the rnd, before blocking.

LEG

CO 63 sts onto 1 needle. Divide sts evenly onto 3 needles (21 sts each needle). Join for working in the rnd, being careful not to twist sts, and place marker (pm) after first st to denote beg of rnd.

Cuff: Work k2, p1 ribbing for 20 rnds—piece should measure 1¾" (4.5 cm) from beg.
Leg: Work Rnd 1 of shell patt for leg (see below), inc 1 st at end of rnd—64 sts. Work

through Rnd 10 of patt, then work Rnds 1–10 six more times (7 reps total)—piece should measure about 8" (20.5 cm) from beg.

HEEL

Heel flap: Sl the first 27 sts onto 2 needles to work later for instep (first and last sts of instep should be purl sts). Turn, and work 1 row on 37 heel sts as foll, dec 7 sts as foll: (WS) Sl 1, [p3, p2tog] 6 times, p2tog, p4—30 sts rem.

Row 1: (RS) *Sl, k1; rep from *.
Row 2: (WS) Sl 1, p29.

Rep Rows 1 and 2 twelve more times, ending with a WS row—26 heel flap rows have been worked; 13 chain sts (slipped selvedge sts) along each side of heel flap.

Turn heel: Cont in short rows as foll:

Row 1: (RS) Sl 1, k16, sl 1, k1, psso, k1, turn.
Row 2: (WS) Sl 1, p5, p2tog, p1, turn.
Row 3: Sl 1, knit to 1 st before gap made on previous row, sl 1, k1, psso, k1, turn.
Row 4: Sl 1, purl to 1 st before gap made on pervious row, p2tog, p1, turn.

Rep Rows 3 and 4 until all sts have been worked—18 heel sts rem.

SHELL PATTERN FOR LEG (multiple of 8 sts)

Rnd 1: *P1, yo, k1, p1, sl 1, k1, psso, k3; rep from *.
Rnd 2: *P1, yo, k2, p1, sl 1, k1, psso, k2; rep from *.
Rnd 3: *P1, yo, k3, p1, sl 1, k1, psso, k1; rep from *.
Rnd 4: *P1, yo, k4, p1, sl 1, k1, psso; rep from *.
Rnd 5: *P1, k5, p1, k1; rep from *.
Rnd 6: *P1, sl 1, k1, psso, k3, p1, yo, k1; rep from *.
Rnd 7: *P1, sl 1, k1, psso, k2, p1, yo, k2; rep from *.
Rnd 8: *P1, sl 1, k1, psso, k1, p1, yo, k3; rep from *.
Rnd 9: *P1, sl 1, k1, psso, p1, yo, k4; rep from *.
Rnd 10: *P1, k1, p1, k5; rep from *.
Repeat Rnds 1–10 for pattern.

Hershey chocolate bar introduced in the U.S.	A.C. Doyle publishes *Adventures of Sherlock Holmes*	X-rays developed in Germany	First kiss on the silver screen	Ice cream cone invented	Lifebuoy soap launched by W. Lever Co.	Aspirin invented by F. Bayer and Co.	First hand-held electric hair dryer	Johann Vaaler patents paper clips	First driving school in England	Upright electric vacuum cleaner	Gas-powered lawn mower

| 1894 | | 1895 | 1896 | | 1897 | 1899 | | 1900 | 1901 | | 1902 |

Gussets: Rejoin for working in the rnd as foll:

Rnd 1: With needle 1, k18 heel sts, then pick up and knit 14 sts along right side of heel flap; with needle 2, work 27 instep sts according to Rnd 1 of shell patt for instep (see below); with needle 3, pick up and knit 14 sts along left side of heel flap, then knit the first 9 sts from needle 1 again—74 sts total; 23 sts each on needles 1 and 3, 27 instep sts on needle 2 have inc'd to 28 sts after completing Rnd 1 of instep patt. Rnd begins at back of heel.

Rnd 2: On needle 1, knit to last 3 sts, k2tog, k1; on needle 2, work instep sts in patt (st counts for each rnd are as given); on needle 3, k1, sl 1, k1, psso, knit to end—1 st dec'd each on needles 1 and 3.

Rnd 3: Work even in patt.

Rep Rnds 2 and 3 seven more times, ending with Rnd 7 of shell patt for instep—59 sts rem; 15 sts each on needles 1 and 3, 29 instep sts after completing Rnd 7 on needle 2.

FOOT

Cont in patt as established until foot measures 6¾" (17 cm) from back of heel, or 2¼" (5.5 cm) less than desired total length, ending with Rnd 10 of shell patt for instep—57 sts; 15 sts each on needles 1 and 3, 27 instep sts after completing Rnd 10 on needle 2. Knit 3 rnds, dec 1 st on last rnd—56 sts rem. Arrange sts so that there are 14 sts each on needles 1 and 3, and 28 instep sts on needle 2.

TOE

Rnd 1: On needle 1, knit to last 3 sts, k2tog, k1; on needle 2, k1, sl 1, k1, psso, knit to last 3 sts, k2tog, k1; on needle 3, k1, sl 1, k1, psso, knit to end—4 sts dec'd.

Rnd 2: Knit.

Rep Rnds 1 and 2 nine more times—16 sts rem; 4 sts each on needles 1 and 3, 8 sts on needle 2. Knit sts from needle 1 onto needle 3—8 sts each on 2 needles. Cut yarn, leaving a 15" (38-cm) tail. Thread tail on a tapestry needle and use the Kitchener st (Glossary, page 117) to graft sts tog. Weave in loose ends. Block on sock blockers or under a damp towel.

SHELL PATTERN FOR INSTEP

Rnd 1: *P1, yo, k1, p1, sl 1, k1, psso, k3; rep from * 2 more times, p1, yo, k1, p1—28 sts.

Rnd 2: *P1, yo, k2, p1, sl 1, k1, psso, k2; rep from * 2 more times, p1, yo, k2, p1—29 sts.

Rnd 3: *P1, yo, k3, p1, sl 1, k1, psso, k1; rep from * 2 more times, p1, yo, k3, p1—30 sts.

Rnd 4: *P1, yo, k4, p1, sl 1, k1, psso; rep from * 2 more times, p1, yo, k4, p1—31 sts.

Rnd 5: *P1, k5, p1, k1; rep from * 2 more times, p1, k5, p1.

Rnd 6: *P1, sl 1, k1, psso, k3, p1, yo, k1; rep from * 2 more times, p1, sl 1, k1, psso, k3, p1—30 sts.

Rnd 7: *P1, sl 1, k1, psso, k2, p1, yo, k2; rep from * 2 more times, p1, sl 1, k1, psso, k2, p1—29 sts.

Rnd 8: *P1, sl 1, k1, psso, k1, p1, yo, k3; rep from * 2 more times, p1, sl 1, k1, psso, k1, p1—28 sts.

Rnd 9: *P1, sl 1, k1, psso, p1, yo, k4; rep from * 2 more times, p1, sl 1, k1, psso, p1—27 sts.

Rnd 10: *P1, k1, p1, k5; rep from * 2 more times, p1, k1, p1.

Repeat Rnds 1–10 for pattern.

First automatic tea maker	Thomas Sullivan invents the tea bag	Electric washing machine launched in the U.S.	Rowenta launches electric iron	Bleriot flies across the English Channel	Neon lighting invented	Coco Chanel launches women's sportswear	Wristwatch becomes popular for men	Deep-freeze invented	In Britain, men over 21 and women over 30 with property allowed to vote	Universal adult suffrage in the U.K. adds women 21 to 30 and abolishes property qualification
1902	1904	1907	1908	1909	1910	1913	1914	1917	1918	1928

GENTLEMAN'S HALF HOSE

in Ringwood Pattern

Weldon's, *Volume 14, Forty-second Series, 1899, page 11*

Original specifies 4 ounces of 4-ply best soft fingering; set of 4 steel #15 (U.S. 000; 1.5 mm) or #16 (U.S. 0000; 1.25 mm) needles.

This pattern has an interesting story. According to page 192 of Richard Rutt's *History of Hand Knitting* (Interweave Press, 2003), in the 1700s Ringwood in Hampshire was "a town of considerable note in the manufacture of stockings." The focus switched to gloves in the 1800s, and these gloves continued to be knitted, mostly in cotton, until 1958 when imported gloves became available at less cost. A pattern for the Ringwood Gloves was published in *Weldon's Practical Needlework*, Volume 20, Series 231, in 1905. According to Rutt, the photo was correct but the pattern was written incorrectly. The pattern I have used for these "Half Hose" appeared correctly in Volume 14 (1899). The original hose from *Weldon's* had a k1, p1 ribbing, which I have switched to k2, p2, a pattern with more stretch that was used in the 1905 gloves from Ringwood. I also added some shaping along the back of the leg—the original had no shaping and looked baggy. I was surprised and pleased by the way the leg pattern extends into the heel flap. I've worked the French Heel as in the original—without slipped stitches during the heel shaping—and changed the toe shaping from a Wedge Toe to a Round Toe.

SPECIFICATIONS

Finished Size 8" (20.5 cm) foot circumference, 11" (28 cm) long from cast-on edge to top of heel flap, and 10½" (26.5 cm) long from back of heel to tip of toe. To fit men's U.S. shoe sizes 9½ to 10½.

Yarn About 555 yd (507 m) of fingering-weight (Super Fine #1) yarn. **We used** Gems Pearl (100% wool; 185 yd [170 m]/50 g; 21 wraps per inch): #50 sage, 3 skeins.

Needles Size 1 (2.5 mm): set of 4 double-pointed. Adjust needle size if necessary to obtain the correct gauge.

Notions Stitch marker (m); tapestry needle.

Gauge 15 sts and 24 rnds = 2" (5 cm) in ringwood st worked in the rnd, before blocking.

LEG

CO 76 sts onto 1 needle. Divide sts as evenly as possible onto 3 needles. Join for working in the rnd, being careful not to twist sts, and place marker (pm) after first st to denote beg of rnd.

Cuff: Work k2, p2 ribbing for 40 rnds —piece should measure about 3¾" (9.5 cm) from beg.

Leg: Knit 2 rnds. Work Rnds 1–3 of ringwood patt (page 67) 4 times (12 ringwood rnds total). *Dec rnd:* (Rnd 1 of patt) Sl 1, k1,

psso, work in patt to last 3 sts, k2tog, p1 (this is the "seam" st)—2 sts dec'd; 74 sts rem. Keeping patt as established and always knitting the first st and the second-to-last st of every rnd, work 9 more rnds even in patt, ending with Rnd 1. Rep dec rnd (Rnd 2 of patt this time), then work 8 rnds even. Rep the last 9 rnds 5 more times, ending with Rnd 1 of patt—62 sts rem. Rep dec rnd— 60 sts rem. Work 14 rnds even in patt, ending with Rnd 1—piece should measure about 11" (28 cm) from beg. Cut yarn.

HEEL

Heel flap: Arrange sts so that 31 sts are on one needle for the heel, with the "seam" st centered on the heel needle. Hold rem 29 sts on 2 needles to work later for instep. Join yarn at beg of heel sts with RS facing. Work 31 heel sts back and forth in rows as foll to cont ringwood patt:

Row 1: (RS) Sl 1, k30.
Row 2: (WS) Sl 1, p30.
Row 3: Sl 1, *p1, k1; rep from *.
Row 4: Sl 1, p30.
Row 5: Sl 1, k30.
Row 6: Sl 1, *k1, p1; rep from *.

Rep Rows 1–6 a total of 3 times, then rep Rows 1 and 2 only 4 times—18 rows ringwood patt, foll by 8 rows of St st.

Turn heel: Work short rows as foll:

Row 1: (RS) K17, sl 1, k1, psso, k1, turn.
Row 2: (WS) P5, p2tog, p1, turn.
Row 3: Knit to 1 st before gap made on previous row, sl 1, k1, psso, k1, turn.
Row 4: Purl to 1 st before gap made on previous row, p2tog, p1, turn.

Hershey chocolate bar introduced in the U.S.	A.C. Doyle publishes *Adventures of Sherlock Holmes*	X-rays developed in Germany	First kiss on the silver screen	Ice cream cone invented	Lifebuoy soap launched by W. Lever Co.	Aspirin invented by F. Bayer and Co.	First hand-held electric hair dryer	Johann Vaaler patents paper clips	First driving school in England	Upright electric vacuum cleaner	Gas-powered lawn mower
1894		1895	1896		1897	1899		1900	1901		1902

> **RINGWOOD PATTERN**
> (multiple of 2 sts)
> *Rnd 1:* *K1, p1; rep from *.
> *Rnds 2 and 3:* Knit.
> Rep Rnds 1–3 for pattern.

Rep Rows 3 and 4 until all sts have been worked, ending with Row 4—17 sts rem.

Gussets: Rejoin for working in the rnd as foll:

Rnd 1: With needle 1, k17 heel sts, then pick up and knit 15 sts along right side of heel flap; with needle 2, work 29 instep sts in patt; with needle 3, pick up and knit 15 sts along left side of heel flap, then knit the first 8 heel sts from needle 1 again—76 sts total; 24 sts on needle 1, 29 instep sts on needle 2, and 23 sts on needle 3. Rnd begins at back of heel.

Rnd 2: On needle 1, knit to last 3 sts, k2tog, k1; on needle 2, work instep sts as established; on needle 3, k1, sl 1, k1, psso, knit to end—2 sts dec'd.

Rnd 3: Knit all sts on needle 1; work instep sts in ringwood patt as established on needle 2; knit all sts on needle 3.

Rep Rnds 2 and 3 five more times—64 sts rem; 18 sts on needle 1, 29 instep sts on needle 2, 17 sts on needle 3.

FOOT

Cont even as established until foot measures 7½" (19 cm) from back of heel, or 3" (7.5 cm) less than desired total length, ending with Rnd 3 of ringwood patt. Knit all sts for 2 rnds.

TOE

Dec Rnd 1: *K6, k2tog; rep from *—56 sts rem.

Knit 6 rnds even.

Dec Rnd 2: *K5, k2tog; rep from *—48 sts rem.

Knit 5 rnds even.

Dec Rnd 3: *K4, k2tog; rep from *—40 sts rem.

Knit 4 rnds even.

Dec Rnd 4: *K3, k2tog; rep from *—32 sts rem.

Knit 3 rnds even.

Dec Rnd 5: *K2, k2tog; rep from *—24 sts rem.

Knit 2 rnds even.

Dec Rnd 6: *K1, k2tog; rep from *—16 sts rem.

Knit 1 rnd even.

Dec Rnd 7: *K2tog; rep from *—8 sts rem.

Cut off yarn, thread tail through a tapestry needle, draw tail through rem sts, and pull up snugly to close end of toe. Weave in loose ends. Block on sock blockers or under a damp towel.

First automatic tea maker	Thomas Sullivan invents the tea bag	Electric washing machine launched in the U.S.	Rowenta launches electric iron	Bleriot flies across the English Channel	Neon lighting invented	Coco Chanel launches women's sportswear	Wristwatch becomes popular for men	Deep-freeze invented	In Britain, men over 21 and women over 30 with property allowed to vote	Universal adult suffrage in the U.K. adds women 21 to 30 and abolishes property qualification
1902	1904	1907	1908	1909	1910	1913	1914	1917	1918	1928

GENTLEMAN'S SOCK

for Evening Wear

Weldon's, *Volume 15, Forty-eighth Series,*
1900, page 7

*Original specifies 4 ounces of 3-ply fingering wool or 2
balls of Empress Knitting Silk (suggested colors are tan,
crimson, or black); four steel #14 (U.S. 00; 1.75 mm)
and four steel #16 (U.S. 0000; 1.25 mm) needles.*

I was attracted to this man's stocking for the decorative pattern down the front of the leg and along the top of the foot. While the pattern is fussy, I think it's appropriate for an "evening sock." I have followed the directions from *Weldon's* as closely as possible, but I've used larger needles than originally called for and have changed the stitch count accordingly. There are a number of mistakes in the original stocking, most notably in the openwork pattern that runs along the foot, which I have corrected here. This sock has a French Heel and Star Toe of Three Points.

SPECIFICATIONS

Finished Size 8" (20.5 cm) foot circumference, 10¼" (26 cm) long from cast-on edge to top of heel flap, and 10¼" (26 cm) long from back of heel to tip of toe. To fit men's U.S. shoe sizes 9 to 10.

Yarn About 591 yd (540 m) of fingering-weight (Super Fine #1) yarn. **We used** Heirloom Argyle (80% wool, 20% nylon; 197 yd [180 m]/50 g; 22 wraps per inch): #488 burgundy heather, 3 skeins.

Needles Leg and foot—size 1 (2.25 mm): set of 4 double-pointed. Toe—size 0 (2 mm): set of 4 double-pointed. Adjust needle size if necessary to obtain the correct gauge.

Notions Stitch marker (m); tapestry needle.

Gauge 17 sts and 24 rnds = 2" (5 cm) in St st worked in the rnd on larger needles, before blocking.

LEG

With yarn doubled, CO 76 sts onto 1 needle. Divide sts as evenly as possible on 3 dpn. Join for working the rnd, being careful not to twist sts, and place marker (pm) after first st to denote beg of rnd. Cut off extra strand of yarn; cont with single strand. **Cuff:** Work k1, p1 ribbing for 30 rnds—piece should measure 3" (7.5 cm) from beg. **Leg:** Knit to end of rnd, M1 (Glossary, page 115)—77 sts. The new st is the "seam" st at the back of the leg, and will be purled every rnd throughout the leg. Work 10 rnds

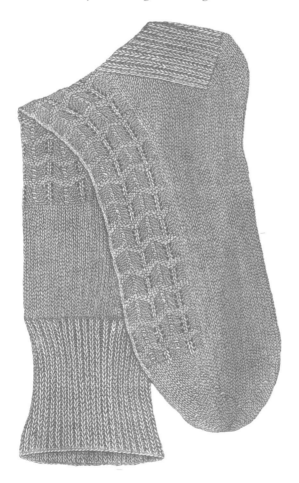

even, purling the seam st and knitting the rem sts. *Dec rnd:* Sl 1, k1, psso, knit to 2 sts before seam st, k2tog, p1 (seam st)—75 sts rem. Work 8 rnds even. Rep dec rnd—73 sts rem. Work 10 rnds even—piece should measure about 5½" (14 cm) from beg. Arrange sts so that there are 18 sts on needle 1, 36 sts on needle 2, and 19 sts on needle 3 (the last st on needle 3 is the seam st). Establish leg patt on front of sock as foll: On needle 1, k18; on needle 2, k2, work Rnd 1 of leg patt (page 71) over center 32 sts, k2; on needle 3, k18, p1 (seam st). Cont as established, working leg patt over center 32 sts until the 8-rnd patt has been worked 7 times total, ending last rnd at end of needle 2 (do not work sts on needle 3)—piece should measure about 10¼" (26 cm) from beg.

HEEL

Set up for working heel sts on 1 needle as foll: (RS) Work 19 sts from needle 3 by working [sl 1, k1] 9 times, p1 (seam st), then work 18 sts of needle 1 onto the same needle by working [sl 1, k1] 9 times—37 heel sts. Hold rem 36 sts on 2 needles to be worked later for instep. Work 37 heel sts back and forth in rows as foll:

Row 1: (WS) Sl 1, p17, k1, p18.
Row 2: (RS) [Sl 1, k1] 9 times, p1, [sl 1, k1] 9 times.
Rep Rows 1 and 2 until a total of 44 rows have been worked, including the initial heel row, ending with Row 1 (WS)—22 chain sts (slipped selvedge sts) along each edge of heel flap.
Turn heel: Work short rows as foll:
Row 1: (RS) Sl 1, k22, k2tog, k1, turn.
Row 2: (WS) Sl 1, p10, p2tog, p1, turn.

Hershey chocolate bar introduced in the U.S.	A.C. Doyle publishes *Adventures of Sherlock Holmes*	X-rays developed in Germany	First kiss on the silver screen	Ice cream cone invented	Lifebuoy soap launched by W. Lever Co.	Aspirin invented by F. Bayer and Co.	First hand-held electric hair dryer	Johann Vaaler patents paper clips	First driving school in England	Upright electric vacuum cleaner	Gas-powered lawn mower
1894		1895	1896		1897	1899		1900	1901		1902

LEG PATTERN (worked over 32 sts)
Rnds 1, 3, and 5: P1, sl 1, k1, psso, [yo, k1, yo, k2, sl 1, k2tog, psso, k2] 3 times, yo, k1, yo, k1, k2tog, p1.
Rnds 2 and 4: P1, k30, p1.
Rnds 6 and 7: Purl.
Rnd 8: P1, k30, p1.
Repeat Rnds 1–8 for pattern.

Row 3: Sl 1, knit to 1 st before gap made by previous row, k2tog, k1, turn.
Row 4: Sl 1, purl to 1 st before gap made by previous row, p2tog, p1, turn.
Rep Rows 3 and 4 until all sts have been worked—23 sts rem.

Shape gussets: Rejoin for working in the rnd as foll:

Rnd 1: With needle 1, k21 heel sts, k2tog, then pick up and knit 22 sts along right side of heel flap; with needle 2, work 36 instep sts in established patt; with needle 3, pick up and knit 22 sts along left side of heel flap, then knit the first 11 sts from needle 1 again—102 sts total; 33 sts each on needles 1 and 3, 36 instep sts on needle 2. Rnd begins at back of heel.

Rnd 2: On needle 1, knit to last 3 sts, k2tog, k1; on needle 2, work instep sts as established; on needle 3, k1, sl 1, k1, psso, knit to end—2 sts dec'd.

Rnd 3: On needle 1, knit; on needle 2, work sts as established; on needle 3, knit.

Rep Rnds 2 and 3 fourteen more times—72 sts rem; 18 sts each on needles 1 and 3, 36 instep sts on needle 2.

FOOT
Cont as established until foot measures 7¾" (19.5 cm) from back of heel, or 2½"

(6.5 cm) less than desired total length. Knit all sts for 4 rnds.

TOE
Rnd 1: *P2tog, k22; rep from *—69 sts rem.
Rnds 2 and 3: Knit.
Rnd 4: *K1, p2tog, k18, p2tog; rep from *—63 sts rem.
Rnds 5 and 6: Knit.
Rnd 7: *K2, p2tog, k14, p2tog, k1; rep from *—57 sts rem.
Rnds 8 and 9: Knit.
Rnd 10: *K3, p2tog, k10, p2tog, k2; rep from *—51 sts rem.
Rnds 11 and 12: Knit.
Rnd 13: *K4, p2tog, k6, p2tog, k3; rep from *—45 sts rem.
Rnds 14 and 15: Knit.
Rnd 16: *K5, p2tog, k2, p2tog, k4; rep from *—39 sts rem.
Rnds 17 and 18: Knit.
Rnd 19: *K6, p2tog, k5; rep from *— 36 sts rem.
Rnds 20 and 21: Knit.
Rnd 22: *K5, p3tog, k4; rep from *—30 sts rem.
Rnd 23: Knit.
Rnd 24: *K4, p3tog, k3; rep from *—24 sts rem.
Rnd 25: Knit.
Rnd 26: *K3, p3tog, k2; rep from *—18 sts rem.
Rnd 27: Knit.
Rnd 28: *K2, p3tog, k1; rep from *—12 sts rem.
Rnd 29: *K2tog, k2—9 sts rem.
Cut yarn, leaving a 12" (30.5-cm) tail. Thread tail on a tapestry needle, draw yarn through rem sts, and pull up snugly to close end of toe. Weave in loose ends. Block on sock blockers or under a damp towel.

First automatic tea maker	Thomas Sullivan invents the tea bag	Electric washing machine launched in the U.S.	Rowenta launches electric iron	Bleriot flies across the English Channel	Neon lighting invented	Coco Chanel launches women's sportswear	Wristwatch becomes popular for men	Deep-freeze invented	In Britain, men over 21 and women over 30 with property allowed to vote	Universal adult suffrage in the U.K. adds women 21 to 30 and abolishes property qualification
1902	1904	1907	1908	1909	1910	1913	1914	1917	1918	1928

EVENING STOCKINGS

for a Young Lady

Weldon's, *Volume 15, Fiftieth Series, 1900, page 5*

Original specifies 3½ ounces of Silkensheen by J. and J. Baldwin; four steel #15 (U.S. 000; 1.5 mm) needles.

This stocking was originally designed to come above the knee, but I have reworked it as a long sock, 12" (30.5 cm) above the heel flap. I've used the same number of rows in the ribbing and kept the pattern as close to the original as possible, placing fewer stitches in the leg and therefore fewer decreases down the leg to the ankle. From there, I have followed the pattern as it was written, working a Dutch Heel and Round Toe variation. The original heel flap is longer than usual, but I've kept it that way because I wanted to see how it worked out. Lovely.

SPECIFICATIONS

Finished Size 7" (18 cm) foot circumference, 12" (30.5 cm) long from cast-on edge to top of heel flap, and 9" (23 cm) long from back of heel to tip of toe. To fit women's U.S. shoe sizes 6½ to 7½.

Yarn About 549 yd (502 m) of fingering-weight (Super Fine #1) yarn. **We used** The Alpaca Yarn Company Glimmer (97% baby alpaca, 3% polyester; 183 yd [167 m]/50 g; 23 wraps per inch): #0100 natural, 3 skeins.

Needles Size 1 (2.5 mm): set of 4 double-pointed. Adjust needle size if necessary to obtain the correct gauge.

Notions Stitch marker (m); tapestry needle.

Gauge 16 sts and 22 rnds = 2" (5 cm) in St st worked in the rnd, before blocking.

LEG

With yarn doubled, CO 75 sts onto 1 needle. Divide sts evenly on 3 needles (25 sts each needle). Join for working in the rnd, being careful not to twist sts, and place marker (pm) after first st to denote beg of rnd. Cut off extra strand of yarn; cont with single strand.

Cuff: Work k2, p1 ribbing for 32 rnds—piece should measure 3" (7.5 cm) from beg.

Leg: K6, p1, [k5, p1] 10 times, k6, p2. Rep the last rnd 7 more times. On the next rnd, establish openwork patt as foll: K6, work Rnd 1 of openwork patt (page 75) over 61 sts, k6, p2. Work in patts as established until 14 rnds of openwork patt have been completed, ending with Rnd 4. On the next rnd (Rnd 5 of openwork patt), work as established to last 2 sts, p2tog—74 sts rem.

Rnd 1: Sl 1, k1, psso, k4, work Rnd 1 of openwork patt over 61 sts, k4, k2tog, p1—72 sts rem.

Rnds 2–10: K5, work 61 sts in openwork patt, k5, p1.

Rnd 11: Sl 1, k1, psso, k3, work 61 sts in openwork patt, k3, k2tog, p1—70 sts rem.

Rnds 12–20: K4, work 61 sts in openwork patt, k4, p1.

Rnd 21: Sl 1, k1, psso, k2, work 61 sts in openwork patt, k2, k2tog, p1—68 sts rem.

Rnds 22–30: K3, work 61 sts in openwork patt, k3, p1.

Rnd 31: Sl 1, k1, psso, k1, work 61 sts in openwork patt, k1, k2tog, p1—66 sts rem.

Rnds 32–40: K2, work 61 sts in openwork patt, k2, p1.

Rnd 41: Sl 1, k1, psso, work 61 sts in openwork patt, k2tog, p1—64 sts rem.

Rnds 42–50: K1, work 61 sts in openwork patt, k1, p1.

Rnd 51: Sl 1, k1, psso, k1, k2tog, yo, k2, work 54 sts in openwork patt (omit the "plus 1" purl st at end), k2tog, p1—62 sts rem.

Rnd 52: K6, [p1, k5] 9 times, k1, p1.

Rnd 53: K1, k2tog, yo, k1, yo, sl 1, k1, psso, [p1, k2tog, yo, k1, yo, sl 1, k1, psso] 9 times, k1, p1.

Rnds 54 and 55: Rep Rnd 52.

Rnd 56: K2, k2tog, yo, k2, [p1, k1, k2tog, yo, k2] 9 times, k1, p1.

Rnds 57–60: Rep Rnds 52–55.

Rnd 61: K2, k2tog, yo, k2, [p1, k1, k2tog, yo, k2] 9 times, sl 1, temporarily remove end-of-rnd marker, p2tog (last st of this rnd tog with first st of next rnd), psso—60 sts rem. The double dec st just worked is the new first st of the rnd; mark this st with end-of-rnd marker.

Rnds 62–84: Work the 6-st rep of openwork patt 10 times around, omitting the "plus 1" purl st at end of patt.

Rnd 85: (Rnd 5 of openwork patt) Work in patt to last 15 sts of rnd—twenty 5-rnd reps of openwork patt completed (except for last 15 unworked sts); piece should measure about 12" (30.5 cm) from CO.

HEEL

Heel flap: Work last 15 sts of rnd as foll: Sl 1, k2, [p1, k5] 2 times, then with same needle [p1, k5] 2 more times, p1, k3—31 sts on heel needle. Hold rem 29 sts on 2 needles to be worked later for instep. Work 31 heel sts back and forth in rows as foll:

Row 1: (WS) Sl 1, p2, [k1, p5] 4 times, k1, p3.

Row 2: (RS) Sl 1, k2, [p1, k5] 4 times, p1, k3.

Rep Rows 1 and 2 eighteen more times, then work Row 1 once more—40 rows total (including initial set-up row); 20 chain sts (slipped selvedge sts) along each edge of heel flap.

Turn heel: Cont in short rows as foll:

Row 1: (RS) Sl 1, k8, [p1, k5] 2 times, p1, sl 1, k1, psso, turn.

Hershey chocolate bar introduced in the U.S.	A.C. Doyle publishes *Adventures of Sherlock Holmes*	X-rays developed in Germany	First kiss on the silver screen	Ice cream cone invented	Lifebuoy soap launched by W. Lever Co.	Aspirin invented by F. Bayer and Co.	First hand-held electric hair dryer	Johann Vaaler patents paper clips	First driving school in England	Upright electric vacuum cleaner	Gas-powered lawn mower
1894		1895	1896		1897	1899		1900	1901		1902

OPENWORK PATTERN

(multiple of 6 sts plus 1)

Rnd 1: *P1, k1, k2tog, yo, k2; rep from * to last st, end, p1.

Rnd 2: *P1, k5; rep from * to last st, end p1.

Rnd 3: *P1, k2tog, yo, k1, yo, sl 1, k1, psso; rep from * to last st, end p1.

Rnds 4 and 5: Rep Rnd 2.

Repeat Rnds 1–5 for pattern.

Row 2: (WS) Sl 1, [k1, p5] 2 times, k1, p2tog, turn.

Row 3: Sl 1, [p1, k5] 2 times, p1, sl 1, k1, psso, turn.

Rep Rows 2 and 3 until all sts have been used, ending with a WS row—15 heel sts rem.

Gussets: Rejoin for working in the rnd as foll:

Rnd 1: With needle 1, work heel sts as foll: sl 1, k6, k2tog, k6, then pick up and knit 21 sts along right side of heel flap; with needle 2, k2, work 25 sts according to Rnd 1 of openwork patt, k2; with needle 3, pick up and knit 21 sts along left side of heel flap, then knit the first 7 sts from needle 1 again—85 sts total; 28 sts each on needles 1 and 3, 29 instep sts on needle 2. Rnd begins at back of heel.

Rnd 2: On needle 1, knit all sts; on needle 2, k2, work 25 sts in openwork patt, k2; on needle 3, knit all sts.

Rnd 3: On needle 1, knit to last 4 sts, k2tog, k2; on needle 2, k2, work 25 sts in openwork patt, k2; on needle 3, k2, sl 1, k1, psso, knit to end—2 sts dec'd.

Rep Rnds 2 and 3 eleven more times, ending with Rnd 5 of openwork patt—61 sts rem; 16 sts each on needles 1 and 3, 29 instep sts on needle 2.

FOOT

Cont even as established for 40 more rnds, ending with Rnd 5 of openwork patt, and working the last 2 sts of the last rnd as k2tog—60 sts; 16 sts on needle 1, 29 instep sts on needle 2, 15 sts on needle 3. Thirteen 5-rnd reps of openwork patt have been worked from the gusset pick-up rnd; foot measures about 7¼" (18.5 cm) from back of heel, or 1¾" (4.5 cm) less than desired total length.

TOE

Rnd 1: *K2tog, k4; rep from *—50 sts rem.

Rnds 2–5: Knit.

Rnd 6: *K2tog, k3; rep from *—40 sts rem.

Rnds 7–9: Knit.

Rnd 10: *K2tog, k2; rep from *—30 sts rem.

Rnds 11 and 12: Knit.

Rnd 13: *K2tog, k1; rep from *—20 sts rem.

Rnds 14 and 15: Knit.

Rnd 16: *K2tog; rep from *—10 sts rem.

Cut yarn leaving a 12" (30.5-cm) tail. Thread tail on a tapestry needle, draw tail through rem sts, and pull up snugly to close end of toe. Weave in loose ends. Block on sock blockers or under a damp towel.

First automatic tea maker	Thomas Sullivan invents the tea bag	Electric washing machine launched in the U.S.	Rowenta launches electric iron	Bleriot flies across the English Channel	Neon lighting invented	Coco Chanel launches women's sportswear	Wristwatch becomes popular for men	Deep-freeze invented	In Britain, men over 21 and women over 30 with property allowed to vote	Universal adult suffrage in the U.K. adds women 21 to 30 and abolishes property qualification
1902	1904	1907	1908	1909	1910	1913	1914	1917	1918	1928

FANCY SILK SOCK

for a Child of 5 or 6 Years

Weldon's, Volume 15, Fiftieth Series, 1900, page 10

Original specifies Lustrine (a silk substitute) by Vicar and Poirson, London; four steel #15 (U.S. 000; 1.5 mm) needles.

This is another *Weldon's* design for a child that makes a perfect lady's sock when it is worked with slightly larger needles and twenty-first-century yarn. I have followed the instructions as written through the French Heel. I've added a purl stitch at the end of the instep stitches on the foot to balance the pattern, and to do so I've adjusted the total stitch count before beginning the toe decreases. The original has the stitches drawn together to close the toe, but I prefer the look and feel of a grafted finish (as in a Flat Toe), so I have provided directions for both methods. Choose the one you like best.

SPECIFICATIONS

Finished Size 7" (18 cm) foot circumference, 7½" (19 cm) long from cast-on edge to top of heel flap, and 9½" (24 cm) long from back of heel to tip of toe. To fit women's U.S. shoe sizes 8 to 9.

Yarn About 430 yd (393 m) of fingering-weight (Super Fine #1) yarn. **We used** Lorna's Laces Shepherd Sock (75% wool, 25% nylon; 215 yd [196 m]/2 oz; 21 wraps per inch): #4ns blackberry, 2 skeins.

Needles Size 1 (2.5 mm): set of 4 double-pointed. Adjust needle size if necessary to obtain the correct gauge.

Notions Stitch marker (m); tapestry needle.

Gauge 17 sts and 22 rnds = 2" (5 cm) in St st worked in the rnd, before blocking.

Note

When working the lace patterns, take care not to lose any yarnovers that occur at the end of a needle.

LEG

Loosely (so top edge will scallop) CO 64 sts onto 1 needle. Arrange sts as evenly as possible on 3 needles. Join for working in the rnd, being careful not to twist sts, and place marker (pm) after first st to denote beg of rnd.

Cuff: Work as foll:

Rnd 1: *K2, sl 1, k2tog, psso, k2, yo, k1, yo; rep from *.

Rnd 2: Knit, slipping the last st of the rnd from the end of the third needle to the beg of the first needle, and counting it as the first st of the foll rnd (do not knit it again) to keep the yarnovers aligned vertically, and counting it as the first of the 2 knit sts in the next rep.

Rep these 2 rnds 7 times total—piece should measure about 1" (2.5 cm) from beg.

Leg: Redistribute sts as evenly as possible on 3 needles again, and knit 2 rnds. Cont in fancy patt as foll:

Rnd 1: *P1, k3, p1, k1, yo, k2tog; rep from *.
Rnds 2 and 4: *P1, k3; rep from *.
Rnd 3: *P1, k3, p1, yo, k2tog, k1; rep from *.
Rnd 5, 6, 7, and 8: Rep Rnds 1–4.
Rnd 9: *P1, yo, sl 1, k2tog, psso, yo, p1, k1, yo, k2tog; rep from *.
Rnd 10: *P1, k3; rep from *.
Rnd 11: *P1, k3, p1, yo, k2tog, k1; rep from *.
Rnd 12: *P1, k3; rep from *.

Rep Rnds 1–12 five more times—6 patt reps total; piece should measure about 7½" (19 cm) from beg.

HEEL

Heel flap: Sl the last 36 sts of rnd onto one needle for heel. Hold rem 28 sts on 2 needles to be worked later for instep. Work 36 heel sts back and forth in rows as foll:

Row 1: (WS) Sl 1, *p5, p2tog; rep from *— 31 sts rem.
Row 2: (RS) [Sl 1, k1] 2 times, sl 1, k2tog, [sl 1, k1] 12 times—30 sts rem.
Row 3: Sl 1, p29.
Row 4: *Sl 1, k1; rep from *.

Rep the last 2 rows 15 more times, ending with a RS row—17 chain edge sts (slipped selvedge sts) along each side of heel flap.

Turn heel: Cont in short rows as foll:

Row 1: (WS) Sl 1, p18, p2tog, p1, turn.
Row 2: (RS) Sl 1, k9, k2tog, k1, turn.
Row 3: Sl 1, purl to 1 st before gap made by last row, p2tog, p1, turn.
Row 4: Sl 1, knit to 1 st before gap made by last row, k2tog, k1, turn.

Rep Rows 3 and 4 until all sts have been worked, ending with a RS row—20 heel sts rem.

Gussets: Rejoin for working in the rnd as foll:

Rnd 1: With needle containing heel sts (needle 1), pick up and knit 17 sts along right side of heel flap; with needle 2, work first 28 instep sts in fancy patt as established (Rnd 1 of patt), M1 pwise (Glossary, page 115; purl this st hereafter to balance patt on instep); with needle 3, pick up and knit 17 sts along left side of heel flap, then knit the first 10 sts from heel needle again—83 sts total; 27 heel sts each on needles 1 and 3, 29 instep sts on needle 2. Rnd begins at back of heel.

Hershey chocolate bar introduced in the U.S.	A.C. Doyle publishes *Adventures of Sherlock Holmes*	X-rays developed in Germany	First kiss on the silver screen	Ice cream cone invented	Lifebuoy soap launched by W. Lever Co.	Aspirin invented by F. Bayer and Co.	First hand-held electric hair dryer	Johann Vaaler patents paper clips	First driving school in England	Upright electric vacuum cleaner	Gas-powered lawn mower
1894		1895	1896		1897	1899		1900	1901		1902

Rnd 2: On needle 1, k1, k2tog, k20, k2tog, k2; on needle 2, work instep sts in patt as established; on needle 3, k2, sl 1, k1, psso, k20, k2tog, k1—79 sts rem.

Rnd 3: Knit sts on needles 1 and 3; work sts in patt as established on needle 2.

Rnd 4: On needle 1, knit to last 4 sts, k2tog, k2; on needle 2, work instep sts as established; on needle 3, k2, sl 1, k1, psso, knit to end—2 sts dec'd.

Rep Rnds 3 and 4 eight more times—61 sts rem; 16 sts each on needles 1 and 3, 29 instep sts on needle 2. Cont even as established until foot measures 7½" (19 cm) from back of heel, or 2" (5 cm) less than desired total length.

TOE

Redistribute sts as foll: Sl last st of needle 1 to needle 2, and sl first st of needle 3 to needle 2—61 sts; 15 sts each on needles 1 and 3, 31 sts on needle 2. Work 1 rnd as foll: Knit to last 2 sts of needle 2, k2tog, knit to end—60 sts; 15 sts each on needles 1 and 3, 30 sts on needle 2. Work toe decreases as foll:

Rnd 1: On needle 1, knit to last 3 sts, k2tog, k1; on needle 2, k1, sl 1, k1, psso, knit to last 3 sts, k2tog, k1; on needle 3, k1, sl 1, k1, psso, knit to end—4 sts dec'd.

Rnd 2: Knit.

Rep Rnds 1 and 2 twelve more times—8 sts rem. Cut yarn, thread tail on a tapestry needle, draw tail through rem sts, and pull up snugly to close end of toe.

For an alternate toe finish, rep Rnds 1 and 2 until 20 sts rem, divide these sts evenly on 2 needles, and with yarn threaded on a tapestry needle, use the Kitchener st (Glossary, page 117) to graft sts tog. Weave in loose ends. Block on sock blockers or under a damp towel.

First automatic tea maker	Thomas Sullivan invents the tea bag	Electric washing machine launched in the U.S.	Rowenta launches electric iron	Bleriot flies across the English Channel	Neon lighting invented	Coco Chanel launches women's sportswear	Wristwatch becomes popular for men	Deep-freeze invented	In Britain, men over 21 and women over 30 with property allowed to vote	Universal adult suffrage in the U.K. adds women 21 to 30 and abolishes property qualification
1902	1904	1907	1908	1909	1910	1913	1914	1917	1918	1928

GENTLEMAN'S FANCY SOCK

Weldon's, *Volume 16, Ninth Series, 1901, page 14*

Original pattern specifies 4 ounces of gray hosiery yarn, AA Peacock quality; ½ ounce of white yarn for the heel and toe; four steel #15 (U.S. 000; 1.5 mm) needles.

Not illustrated in *Weldon's*, this pattern nonetheless intrigued me so much that I knitted it. Thinking it might be a good man's pattern, I've used a very fine yarn at 9 stitches to the inch on size 0 (2 mm) needles. To keep the sock fancy, I haven't used the contrasting color in the French Heel and Wide Toe that's specified in the original pattern. My yarn is hand-dyed and available in one-of-a-kind colors from Schaefer Yarns.

SPECIFICATIONS

Finished Size 7½" (19 cm) foot circumference, 8½" (21.5 cm) long from cast-on edge to top of heel flap, and 10½" (26.5 cm) long from back of heel to tip of toe. To fit men's U.S. shoe sizes 9½ to 10½.

Yarn About 560 yd (512 m) of fingering-weight (Super Fine #1) yarn. **We used** Schaefer Yarns Anne (60% superwash merino wool, 25% mohair, 15% nylon; 560 yd [512 m]/4 oz; 25 wraps per inch): khaki green, 1 skein.

Needles Size 0 (2 mm): set of 4 double-pointed. Adjust needle size if necessary to obtain the correct gauge.

Notions Stitch marker (m); tapestry needle.

Gauge 18 sts and 24 rows = 2" (5 cm) in St st worked in the rnd, before blocking.

LEG

CO 80 sts onto 1 needle. Divide sts as evenly as possible on 3 needles. Join for working in the rnd, being careful not to twist sts, and place marker (pm) after first st to denote beg of rnd.

Cuff: Work k2, p2 ribbing for 20 rnds—piece should measure 1½" (3.8 cm) from beg.

Leg: Knit 2 rnds. Cont in patt as foll:

Rnds 1–8: *P2, k2; rep from *.

Rnds 9 and 10: Knit.

Rnds 11–18: *K2, p2; rep from *.

Rnd 19: Knit.

Rnd 20: K9, sl 1, k1, psso, k2tog, knit to end—78 sts; center back leg will be between the 2 decs from now until Rnd 50.

Rnds 21–28: P2, k2, p2, k3, p2 (center back leg), k3, *p2, k2; rep from * to end.

Rnd 29: Knit.

Rnd 30: K8, sl 1, k1, psso, k2tog, knit to end—76 sts.

Rnds 31–38: *K2, p2; rep from *.

Rnd 39: Knit.

Rnd 40: K7, k2tog, sl 1, k1, psso, knit to end—74 sts.

Rnds 41–48: P2, k2, p2, k4, *p2, k2; rep from * to end.

Rnd 49: Knit.

Rnd 50: K6, k2tog, sl 1, k1, psso, knit to end—72 sts.

Rnds 51–58: *K2, p2; rep from *.

Rnds 59 and 60: Knit.

Rnds 61–68: *P2, k2; rep from *.

Rnds 69 and 70: Knit.

Rnds 71–88: Rep Rnds 51–68.

Rnd 89: Knit.

Rnd 90: K7, M1 pwise (Glossary, page 115), knit to end—73 sts; piece should measure about 8½" (21.5 cm) from beg. The new st is the "seam st" and will be purled every row for the heel flap.

HEEL

Heel flap:

Row 1: (RS) K7, p1, k17, turn.

Row 2: (WS) Sl 1, p16, k1, p17, turn—35 sts on one needle for heel; seam st is at center. Hold rem 38 sts on 2 needles to be worked later for instep. Work 35 heel sts back and forth in rows as foll:

Row 3: Sl 1, k16, p1, k17.

Row 4: Sl 1, p16, k1, p17.

Rep Rows 3 and 4 until a total of 32 rows have been worked for heel flap, ending with a WS row—16 chain sts (slipped selvedge sts) at each edge of heel flap.

Turn heel: Work short rows as foll:

Row 1: (RS) Sl 1, k17, sl 1, k1, psso, k1, turn.

Row 2: (WS) Sl 1, p2, p2tog, p1, turn.

Row 3: Sl 1, knit to 1 st before gap made on previous row, sl 1, k1, psso, k1, turn.

Row 4: Sl 1, purl to 1 st before gap made on previous row, p2tog, p1, turn.

Rep Rows 3 and 4 until all sts have been worked, ending with a WS row—19 heel sts rem.

Gussets: Rejoin for working in the rnd as foll:

Rnd 1: With needle 1, k19 heel sts, then pick up and knit 18 sts along right side of heel flap; with needle 2, work 38 instep sts in patt as established; with needle 3, pick up and knit 17 sts along left side of heel flap, then knit the first 10 heel sts from needle 1 again—92 sts total; 27 sts each on needles 1 and 3, 38 instep sts on needle 2. Rnd begins at back of heel.

Rnd 2: On needle 1, knit to last 3 sts, k2tog, k1; on needle 2, work instep sts in patt; on needle 3, k1, sl 1, k1, psso, knit to end—2 sts dec'd.

Rnd 3: Knit sts on needles 1 and 3, work instep patt as established on needle 2.

Hershey chocolate bar introduced in the U.S.	A.C. Doyle publishes *Adventures of Sherlock Holmes*	X-rays developed in Germany	First kiss on the silver screen	Ice cream cone invented	Lifebuoy soap launched by W. Lever Co.	Aspirin invented by F. Bayer and Co.	First hand-held electric hair dryer	Johann Vaaler patents paper clips	First driving school in England	Upright electric vacuum cleaner	Gas-powered lawn mower
1894		1895	1896		1897	1899		1900	1901		1902

Rep Rnds 2 and 3 ten more times—70 sts rem; 16 sts each on needles 1 and 3, 38 instep sts on needle 2.

FOOT

Cont as established until 70 rnds have been completed from beg of gussets (seven 10-row patt blocks), ending with 2 plain knit rnds—foot should measure about 8" (20.5 cm) from back of heel, or 2½" (6.5 cm) less than desired total length.

TOE

Knit 6 rnds even. Sl the first st on needle 2 to the end of needle 1, and sl the last st of needle 2 to the beg of needle 3—17 sts each on needles 1 and 3, 36 instep sts on needle 2. Cont as foll:

Rnd 1: On needle 1, knit to last 4 sts, k2tog, k2; on needle 2, k2, sl 1, k1, psso, knit to last 4 sts, k2tog, k2; on needle 3, k2, sl 1, k1, psso, knit to end—4 sts dec'd.

Rnd 2: Knit.

Rep Rnds 1 and 2 twelve more times—18 sts rem; 4 sts each on needles 1 and 3, 10 instep sts on needle 2. *Next rnd:* K4, k2, sl 1, k1, psso, k2, k2tog, k2, k4—16 sts rem; 4 sts each on needles 1 and 3, 8 instep sts on needle 2. *Next rnd:* Rep Rnd 1 of toe decreases—12 sts rem; 3 sts each on needles 1 and 3, 6 instep sts on needle 2. Sl the first 3 sts from needle 2 onto needle 1, and sl rem sts from needle 2 onto needle 3—6 sts each on 2 needles. Cut yarn, leaving a 15" (38-cm) tail. Thread tail on a tapestry needle and use the Kitchener st (Glossary, page 117) to graft sts tog. Weave in loose ends. Block on sock blockers or under a damp towel.

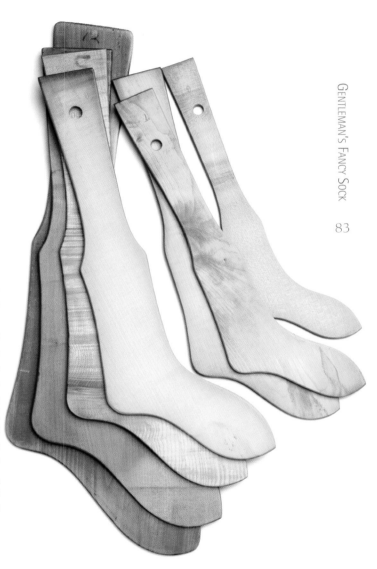

First automatic tea maker	Thomas Sullivan invents the tea bag	Electric washing machine launched in the U.S.	Rowenta launches electric iron	Bleriot flies across the English Channel	Neon lighting invented	Coco Chanel launches women's sportswear	Wristwatch becomes popular for men	Deep-freeze invented	In Britain, men over 21 and women over 30 with property allowed to vote	Universal adult suffrage in the U.K. adds women 21 to 30 and abolishes property qualification
1902	1904	1907	1908	1909	1910	1913	1914	1917	1918	1928

GENTLEMAN'S PLAIN WINTER SOCK

with Dutch Heel

Weldon's, *Volume 16, Ninth Series, 1901, page 5*

Original specifies 4 ounces of 4 super ply fingering wool by Messrs. John Paton, Son & Co., Alloa; four steel #14 (U.S. 00; 1.75 mm) needles.

This sock is one of many very plain, mostly stockinette-stitch socks found in *Weldon's.* I was attracted to the long ribbed cuff and the interesting Dutch Heel shaping. I've worked the sock almost exactly as the pattern was written. The only changes I've made are to go up to a larger needle size and to make mirror decreases in the heel shaping. The original instructions specify "take 2 together," which I read as "k2tog," for both the right and left decrease. I've changed the left decrease to sl 1, k1, psso. The sock ends with a Wide Toe.

SPECIFICATIONS

Finished Size 7¾" (19.5 cm) foot circumference, 9" (23 cm) long from cast-on edge to top of heel flap, and 10" (25.5 cm) long from back of heel to tip of toe. To fit men's U.S. shoe sizes 8 to 9.

Yarn About 394 yd (360 m) of fingering-weight (Super Fine #1) yarn. **We used** Heirloom Argyle (80% wool, 20% nylon; 197 yd [180 m]/50 g; 22 wraps per inch) #491 gray, 2 skeins. *Note:* You'll need 3 skeins if you lengthen the leg or foot.

Needles Size 1 (2.5 mm): set of 4 double-pointed. Adjust needle size if necessary to obtain the correct gauge.

Notions Stitch marker (m); tapestry needle.

Gauge 16 sts and 21 rnds = 2" (5 cm) in St st worked in the rnd, before blocking.

86

LEG

With yarn doubled, CO 70 sts onto 1 needle. Divide sts as evenly as possible onto 3 needles. Join for working in the rnd, being careful not to twist sts, and place marker (pm) after first st to denote beg of rnd. Cut off extra strand of yarn; cont with single strand of yarn.

Cuff: Work k3, p2 ribbing for 46 rnds—piece should measure 4¼" (11 cm) from beg.

Leg: K69, p1. Rep the last rnd 48 more times—49 rnds total; piece should measure about 9" (23 cm) from beg. Arrange sts so that the first 18 sts are on needle 1, the next 33 sts are on needle 2 for instep, and the last 19 sts on needle 3. Knit across sts on needles 1 and 2.

HEEL

Heel flap: Set up for working 37 heel sts on 1 needle as foll: Sl 1, k17, p1 (center st), k18 sts from needle 1—37 sts for heel. Hold rem 33 sts on 2 needles to be worked later for instep. Work 37 heel sts back and forth in rows as foll:

Row 1: (WS) Sl 1, p17, k1 (center st), p18.

Row 2: (RS) Sl 1, k17, p1, k18.

Rep Rows 1 and 2 a total of 11 times, then work Row 1 once more—24 rows total, including the set-up row; 12 chain sts (slipped selvedge sts) along each edge of heel flap. Cont as foll:

Row 25: (RS) Sl 1, k14, k2tog, k1, p1, k1, sl 1, k1, psso, k15—2 sts dec'd.

Rows 26, 28, and 30: Purl to center st, k1, purl to end.

Row 27: Sl 1, k13, k2tog, k1, p1, k1, sl 1, k1, psso, k14—2 sts dec'd.

Row 29: Sl 1, k12, k2tog, k1, p1, k1, sl 1, k1, psso, k13—2 sts dec'd.

Row 31: Sl 1, k11, k2tog, k1, p1, k1, sl 1, k1, psso, k12—29 heel sts rem.

Row 32: Rep Row 26.

Turn heel: Work short rows as foll:

Row 1: (RS) K11, k2tog, k3, sl 1, k1, psso, turn.

Row 2: (WS) Sl 1, p3, p2tog, turn.

Row 3: Sl 1, k3, sl 1, k1, psso, turn.

Rep Rows 2 and 3 until all heel sts have been worked, ending with Row 3—5 heel sts rem.

Gussets: Rejoin for working in the rnd as foll:

Rnd 1: With needle holding 5 heel sts (needle 1), pick up and knit 16 sts along right side of heel flap, k1 from instep needle; with needle 2, work 31 instep sts; with needle 3, k1 (last instep st), pick up and knit 16 sts along left side of heel flap, then knit the first 3 heel sts from needle 1 again—70 sts total; 19 heel sts on needle 1, 31 instep sts on needle 2, 20 heel sts on needle 3. Rnd begins at back of heel.

Rnd 2: Knit to last 3 sts on needle 1, k2tog, k1; k31 instep sts on needle 2; k1, sl 1, k1, psso, knit to end of needle 3—2 sts dec'd.

Rnd 3: Knit.

Rep Rnds 2 and 3 until 62 sts rem—15 heel sts on needle 1, 31 instep sts on needle 2, 16 heel sts on needle 3.

Hershey chocolate bar introduced in the U.S.	A.C. Doyle publishes *Adventures of Sherlock Holmes*	X-rays developed in Germany	First kiss on the silver screen	Ice cream cone invented	Lifebuoy soap launched by W. Lever Co.	Aspirin invented by F. Bayer and Co.	First hand-held electric hair dryer	Johann Vaaler patents paper clips	First driving school in England	Upright electric vacuum cleaner	Gas-powered lawn mower
1894		1895	1896		1897	1899		1900	1901		1902

FOOT

Work even until foot measures 7¾"
(19.5 cm) from back of heel, or 2¼"
(5.5 cm) less than desired total
length.

TOE

Rnd 1: On needle 1, knit to
last 4 sts k2tog, k2; on needle 2, k2, sl 1, k1, psso, knit
to last 4 sts, k2tog, k2; on
needle 3, k2, sl 1, k1, psso, knit
to end—4 sts dec'd.

Rnd 2: Knit.

Rep Rnds 1 and 2 until 22 sts rem. Rep
Rnd 1 twice more (do not work Rnd 2 in
between)—14 sts rem. Cut yarn. Thread tail
on a tapestry needle, draw through rem sts,
and pull up snugly to close end of toe.
Weave in loose ends. Block on sock blockers or under a damp towel.

First automatic tea maker	Thomas Sullivan invents the tea bag	Electric washing machine launched in the U.S.	Rowenta launches electric iron	Bleriot flies across the English Channel	Neon lighting invented	Coco Chanel launches women's sportswear	Wristwatch becomes popular for men	Deep-freeze invented	In Britain, men over 21 and women over 30 with property allowed to vote	Universal adult suffrage in the U.K. adds women 21 to 30 and abolishes property qualification
1902	1904	1907	1908	1909	1910	1913	1914	1917	1918	1928

CHILD'S SOCK

in Miranda Pattern

Weldon's, *Volume 19, Fifty-ninth Series, 1904, page 7*

Original specified Ardern's No 22 Crochet Cotton; four steel #17 (U.S. 00000; 1 mm) needles.

Even though this sock was designed for a child of two to three years old, I loved the pattern and thought it would translate well into an adult's sock. I also thought size 0 (2 mm) needles sounded much better than size 00000 (1 mm)! The design down the leg is made up of squares of openwork patterns. They decrease down the back of the leg for a "shapely" fit and decorate the top of the foot. This sock has a French Heel and a Flat Toe.

SPECIFICATIONS

Finished Size 7½" (19 cm) foot circumference, 8½" (21.5 cm) long from cast-on edge to top of heel flap, and 9½" (24 cm) long from back of heel to tip of toe. To fit women's U.S. shoe sizes 8 to 9.

Yarn About 430 yd (393 m) of fingering-weight (Super Fine #1) yarn. **We used** Lorna's Laces Shepherd Sock (75% wool, 25% nylon; 215 yd [196 m]/2 oz; 21 wraps per inch): #8ns harvest, 2 skeins.

Needles Size 0 (2 mm): set of 4 double-pointed. Adjust needle size if necessary to obtain the correct gauge.

Notions Stitch marker (m); tapestry needle.

Gauge 17 sts and 22 rnds = 2" (5 cm) in St st worked in the round, before blocking.

LEG

CO 80 sts onto 1 needle. Divide sts on 3 needles so that there are 24 sts each on needles 1 and 3, and 32 sts on needle 2. Join for working in the rnd, being careful not to twist sts, and place marker (pm) after first st to denote beg of rnd.

Cuff: Work k2, p2 ribbing for 20 rnds—piece should measure 1½" (3.8 cm) from beg.

Leg: Knit to 1 st before end of rnd, M1 pwise (Glossary, page 115), k1—81 sts; inc'd st is the "seam" st. Move the last st on needle 3 to needle 1, the last st on needle 1 to needle 2, and the last st on needle 2 to needle 3—24 sts on needle 1, 32 sts on needle 2, and 25 sts on needle 3; seam st is now last st of rnd. Purling the seam st every rnd, knit all other sts for 6 rnds. Work Rnds 1–14 of Leg chart (page 91) 2 times. Work Rnds 15–65 once, working decs as indicated—65 sts rem; 16 sts on needle 1, 32 sts on needle 2, 17 sts on needle 3.

HEEL

Heel flap: K16 sts on needle 1, turn work, sl 1, p15, k1 (seam st), p16—33 heel sts. Hold rem 32 sts on 2 needles to be worked later for instep. Work 33 heel sts back and forth in rows as foll:

Row 1: (RS) Sl 1, k15, p1, k16.

Row 2: (WS) Sl 1, p15, k1, p16.

Rep Rows 1 and 2 until a total of 24 rows have been worked, ending with a WS row—12 chain sts (slipped selvedge sts) along each edge of heel flap.

Turn heel: Work short rows as foll:

Row 1: (RS) K18, sl 1, k1, psso, k1, turn.

Row 2: (WS) P5, p2tog, p1, turn.

Row 3: Knit to 1 st before gap made on previous row, sl 1, k1, psso, k1, turn.

Row 4: Purl to 1 st from gap made on previous row, p2tog, p1, turn.

Cont in this manner, working 1 more st before dec every row until all heel sts have been worked, ending with a WS row—19 heel sts rem.

Gussets: Rejoin for working in the rnd as foll:

Rnd 1: With needle 1, k19 heel sts, then pick up and knit 14 sts along right side of heel flap; with needle 2, work Rnd 1 of Foot chart (page 91) across 32 instep sts; with needle 3, pick up and knit 14 sts along left side of heel flap, then knit the first 10 sts from needle 1 again—79 sts total; 23 sts on needle 1, 32 instep sts on needle 2, 24 sts on needle 3. Rnd begins at back of heel.

Rnd 2: On needle 1, knit; on needle 2, work instep sts in established patt; on needle 3, knit.

Rnd 3: On needle 1, knit to last 3 sts, k2tog, k1; on needle 2, work instep sts in established patt; on needle 3, k1, sl 1, k1, psso, knit to end—2 sts dec'd.

Rep Rnds 2 and 3 eight more times—61 sts rem; 14 heel sts on needle 1, 32 instep sts on needle 2, 15 heel sts on needle 3.

FOOT

Cont as established, maintaining patt on instep sts until Rnds 1–14 of Foot chart have been worked 4 times. *Next rnd:* On needle 1, knit; on needle 2, k7, [k2tog, k6] 2 times, k2tog, k7; on needle 3, knit—58 sts rem; 29 sts on needle 2. Knit 8 rnds—foot should measure

Hershey chocolate bar introduced in the U.S.	A.C. Doyle publishes *Adventures of Sherlock Holmes*	X-rays developed in Germany	First kiss on the silver screen	Ice cream cone invented	Lifebuoy soap launched by W. Lever Co.	Aspirin invented by F. Bayer and Co.	First hand-held electric hair dryer	Johann Vaaler patents paper clips	First driving school in England	Upright electric vacuum cleaner	Gas-powered lawn mower
1894		1895	1896		1897	1899		1900	1901		1902

about 7½" (19 cm) from back of heel, or 2" (5 cm) less than desired total length.

TOE

Rnd 1: On needle 1, knit to last 3 sts, k2tog, k1; on needle 2, k1, sl 1, k1, psso, knit to last 3 sts, k2tog, k1; on needle 3, k1, sl 1, k1, psso, knit to end—4 sts dec'd.
Rnd 2: Knit.

Rep Rnds 1 and 2 nine more times—18 sts rem; 4 sts on needle 1, 9 sts on needle 2, 5 sts on needle 3. With needle 3, knit across sts on needle 1—9 sts rem on each of 2 needles. Cut yarn, leaving a 12" (30.5-cm) tail. Thread tail on a tapestry needle and use the Kitchener st (Glossary, page 117) to graft sts tog. Weave in loose ends. Block on sock blockers or under a damp towel.

Foot

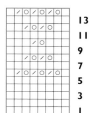

Leg

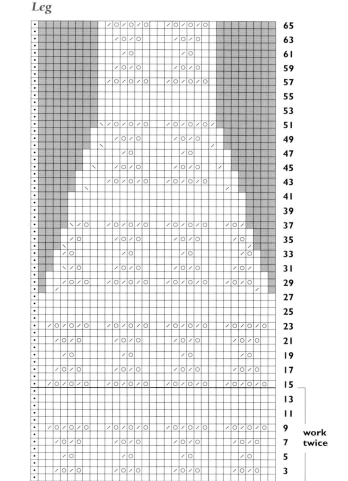

knit

· purl

∕ k2tog

∖ sl 1, k1, psso

○ yo

no stitch

pattern repeat

↑ seam st

work twice

First automatic tea maker	Thomas Sullivan invents the tea bag	Electric washing machine launched in the U.S.	Rowenta launches electric iron	Bleriot flies across the English Channel	Neon lighting invented	Coco Chanel launches women's sportswear	Wristwatch becomes popular for men	Deep-freeze invented	In Britain, men over 21 and women over 30 with property allowed to vote	Universal adult suffrage in the U.K. adds women 21 to 30 and abolishes property qualification
1902	1904	1907	1908	1909	1910	1913	1914	1917	1918	1928

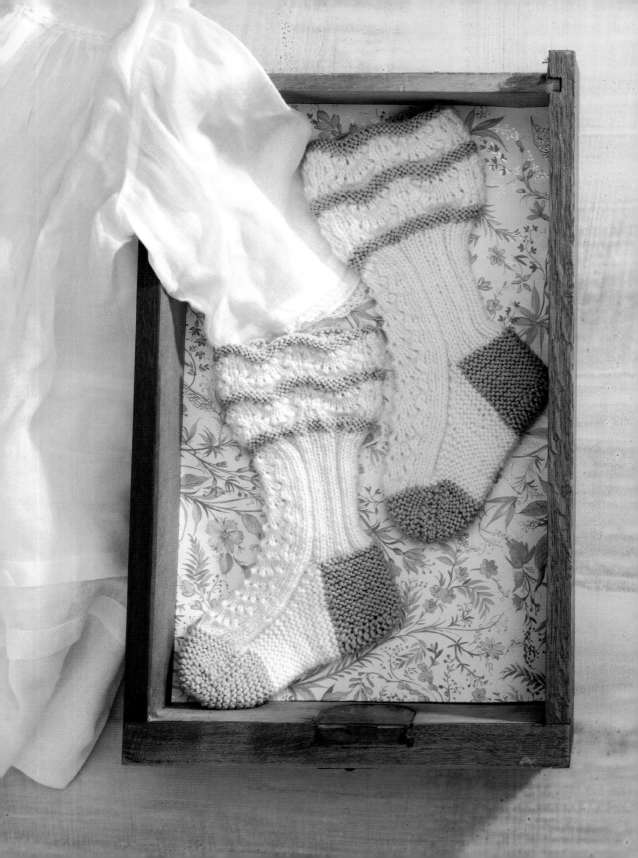

BABY'S
BOOTIKIN

Weldon's, *Volume 20, Sixty-third Series, 1905, page 8*

Original specifies 1½ ounces of Andalusian wool (1 ounce white and ½ ounce blue); four steel #16 (U.S. 0000; 1.25 mm) needles.

Baby's Bootikin is designed for an infant. I have worked the pattern as it was written, including the order in which the gussets are picked up. The first needle is the left side of the heel flap; what we normally designate as the first needle holds the stitches for the right side of the heel and in this case, is the second needle. The instep stitches are on the third needle. I have changed the toe ending from a simple bound-off and sewn seam to a gathered tip, which is tidy and reduces bulk at the toe. This bootikin has a Dutch Heel and a Flat Toe (both worked in garter stitch).

SPECIFICATIONS

Finished Size 4" (10 cm) foot circumference, 5" (12.5 cm) long from cast-on edge to top of heel flap, and 4½" (11.5 cm) long from back of heel to tip of toe. To fit U.S. infants' shoe sizes about 4 to 5.

Yarn About 192 yd (175 m) each of 2 colors of fingering-weight (Super Fine #1) yarn. **We used** Dale of Norway Baby Ull (100% superwash wool; 192 yd [175 m]/50 g; 22 wraps per inch): #0020 natural (MC) and #5303 lavender (CC), 1 ball each.

Needles Size 00 (1.75 mm): set of 4 double-pointed. Adjust needle size if necessary to obtain the correct gauge.

Notions Stitch marker (m); tapestry needle.

Gauge 8 sts and 16 rnds (8 garter ridges) = 1" (2.5 cm) in garter st worked in the rnd, before blocking.

Note

The stitch count varies from round to round in the shell pattern. When worked correctly, each purl stitch will line up directly above a purl stitch in the previous round.

LEG

With CC, CO 60 sts onto 1 needle. Divide sts on 3 needles so that 18 sts are on needle 1, 24 sts are on needle 2, and 18 sts are on needle 3. Join for working in the rnd, being careful not to twist sts, and place marker (pm) after first st to denote beg of rnd.

Cuff: Purl 3 rnds. Cut off CC. Join MC and knit 1 rnd. Work Rnds 1–5 of shell patt for leg (page 95) 2 times. Do not cut off MC. Join CC and knit 1 rnd, then purl 3 rnds. Cut off CC. Cont with MC, knit 1 rnd then work Rnds 1–5 of shell patt for leg 2 more times. Do not cut off MC. *Next rnd:* With CC, *k1, sl 1, k1, psso, k5, k2tog, k2; rep from *—50 sts rem; if necessary, rearrange sts so there are 15 sts each on needles 1 and 3, and 20 sts on needle 2. Cont with CC, purl 3 rnds. Cut off CC.

Leg: With MC only, cont as foll:

Rnd 1: Knit.

Rnd 2: P1, k2, p2, k2tog, [k1, p1] 2 times, k2, p2, k2tog, [k1, p1] 2 times, k7, p1, k1, p1, k2, p2, k2tog, [k1, p1] 2 times, k2, p2, k2tog, k1, p1, k1—46 sts rem; 14 sts on needle 1, 19 sts on needle 2, 13 sts on needle 3.

Rnd 3: P1, k2, p2, k2, p1, k1, p1, k2, p2, k2, [p1, k1] 2 times, [yo, k1] 6 times, [p1, k1, p1, k2, p2, k2] 2 times, p1, k1—52 sts.

Rnd 4: Work 19 sts in established rib, k13, work 20 sts in established rib.

Rnd 5: Work 19 sts in established rib, sl 1, k1, psso, k9, k2tog, work 20 sts in established rib—50 sts rem.

Rnd 6: Work 19 sts in established rib, sl 1, k1, psso, k7, k2tog, work 20 sts in established rib—48 sts rem.

Rnd 7: Work 19 sts in established rib, sl 1, k1, psso, k5, k2tog, work 20 sts in established rib—46 sts rem.

Rep Rnds 3–7 five more times, ending the last rnd 13 sts before the end of the rnd. Cut off MC.

HEEL

Heel flap: With CC, k13 unworked sts at end of rnd on needle 3, and on the same needle, knit the first 12 sts from needle 1—25 heel sts. Hold rem 21 sts on 2 needles to be worked later for instep (first 2 and last 2 sts of instep needle should be purls). Work 25 heel sts back and forth in rows as foll:

Row 1: Sl 1, k24, turn.

Rep this row until a total of 24 rows have been worked, ending with a WS row—12 chain sts (slipped selvedge sts) along each edge of heel flap.

Turn heel: Work short rows as foll:

Row 1: (RS) K16, turn.

Row 2: (WS) Sl 1, k6, turn.

Row 3: Sl 1, k5, k2tog, turn.

Rep Row 3 every row until all heel sts have been worked, ending with a WS row—7 sts rem. Cut off CC.

Hershey chocolate bar introduced in the U.S.	A.C. Doyle publishes *Adventures of Sherlock Holmes*	X-rays developed in Germany	First kiss on the silver screen	Ice cream cone invented	Lifebuoy soap launched by W. Lever Co.	Aspirin invented by F. Bayer and Co.	First hand-held electric hair dryer	Johann Vaaler patents paper clips	First driving school in England	Upright electric vacuum cleaner	Gas-powered lawn mower
1894		1895	1896		1897	1899		1900	1901		1902

SHELL PATTERN FOR LEG

(multiple of 12 sts)

Rnd 1: *P1, sl 1, k1, psso, k5, k2tog, p1, k1; rep from *—multiple of 10 sts.

Rnd 2: *P1, k1, [yo, k1] 6 times, p1, k1; rep from *—multiple of 16 sts.

Rnd 3: *P1, k13, p1, k1; rep from *.

Rnd 4: *P1, sl 1, k1, psso, k9, k2tog, p1, k1; rep from *—multiple of 14 sts.

Rnd 5: *P1, sl 1, k1, psso, k7, k2tog, p1, k1; rep from *—multiple of 12 sts.

Repeat Rnds 1–5 for pattern.

SHELL PATTERN FOR INSTEP (worked over 21 sts)

Rnd 1: P2, k2, [p1, k1] 2 times, [yo, k1] 6 times, p1, k1, p1, k2, p2—27 sts.

Rnd 2: Work 7 sts in established rib, k13, work 7 sts in established rib.

Rnd 3: Work 7 sts in established rib, sl 1, k1, psso, k9, k2tog, work 7 sts in established rib—25 sts.

Rnd 4: Work 7 sts in established rib, sl 1, k1, psso, k7, k2tog, work 7 sts in established rib—23 sts.

Rnd 5: Work 7 sts in established rib, sl 1, k1, psso, k5, k2tog, work 7 sts in established rib—21 sts.

Repeat Rnds 1–5 for pattern.

Gussets: Rejoin MC to the lower edge of the heel flap, ready to pick up sts along the left side of heel flap.

Rnd 1: With MC and needle 1, pick up and knit 14 sts along left side of heel flap, k4 heel sts; with needle 2, knit rem 3 heel sts, then pick up and knit 14 sts along other side of heel flap; with needle 3, work Rnd 1 of shell patt for instep (see above) across 21 instep sts—62 sts total; 18 sts on needle 1, 17 sts on needle 2, 21 instep sts on needle 3 inc'd to 27 sts after Rnd 1 of patt. Rnd begins at end of instep.

Rnd 2: On needles 1 and 2, purl all sts; on needle 3, work instep sts in patt.

Rnd 3: On needle 1, sl 1, k1, psso, knit to end; on needle 2, knit to last 2 sts, k2tog; on needle 3, work instep sts in patt—2 gusset sts dec'd.

Rnd 4: On needles 1 and 2, purl all sts; on needle 3, work instep sts in patt.

Rep Rnds 3 and 4 six more times, ending with Rnd 1 of shell patt for instep—14 sts dec'd for gussets; 48 sts rem; 11 sts on needle 1, 10 sts on needle 2, 27 instep sts on needle 3.

FOOT

Cont in patt with MC until a total of 30 rnds (6 complete reps) of shell patt for instep have been worked from the gusset pick-up rnd, ending with Rnd 5—42 sts; 11 sts on needle 1, 10 sts on needle 2, 21 instep sts on needle 3; foot should measures about 3¼" (8.5 cm) from back of heel, or 1¼" (3.2 cm) less than desired total length. Cut MC.

TOE

With CC, [knit 1 rnd, purl 1 rnd] 4 times (add more rnds here for a longer foot). Cont as foll:

Rnd 1: On needle 1, k1, sl 1, k1, psso, knit to end; on needle 2, knit to last 3 sts, k2tog, k1; on needle 3, k1, sl 1, k1, psso, knit to last 3 sts, k2tog, k1—4 sts dec'd.

Rnd 2: Purl all sts.

Rep Rnds 1 and 2 seven more times—10 sts rem; 3 sts on needle 1, 2 sts on needle 2, 5 instep sts on needle 3. Cut yarn, leaving a 12" (30.5-cm) tail. Thread tail on a tapestry needle, draw through rem sts and pull up snugly to close end of toe. Weave in loose ends. Block on sock blockers or under a damp towel.

	Thomas Sullivan invents the tea bag	Electric washing machine launched in the U.S.	Rowenta launches electric iron	Bleriot flies across the English Channel	Neon lighting invented	Coco Chanel launches women's sportswear	Wristwatch becomes popular for men	Deep-freeze invented	In Britain, men over 21 and women over 30 with property allowed to vote	Universal adult suffrage in the U.K. adds women 21 to 30 and abolishes property qualification
First automatic tea maker										
1902	1904	1907	1908	1909	1910	1913	1914	1917	1918	1928

LITTLE CHILD'S SOCK

Weldon's, *Volume 22, Sixty-eighth Series, 1907, page 13*

Original specifies 2 ounces white merino, Shetland, or 2-ply fingering wool; four steel #16 (U.S. 0000; 1.25 mm) needles.

While this sock was originally designed for a child, larger needles and thicker yarn than called for in *Weldon's* makes it stylish for women. Knit it on even larger needles for a man. The pattern is a collection of knit and purl patterns, almost a sampler of stitches. This sock has a French Heel and Flat Toe.

SPECIFICATIONS

Finished Size 7" (18 cm) foot circumference, 9½" (24 cm) long from cast-on edge to top of heel flap, and 9" (23 cm) long from back of heel to tip of toe. To fit women's U.S. shoe sizes 6½ to 7½.

Yarn About 430 yd (393 m) of fingering-weight (Super Fine #1) yarn. **We used** Lorna's Laces Shepherd Sock (75% wool, 25% nylon; 215 yd [196 m]/2 oz; 21 wraps per inch): #6ns Douglas fir, 2 skeins.

Needles Size 1 (2.5 mm): set of 4 double-pointed. Adjust needle size if necessary to obtain the correct gauge.

Notions Stitch marker (m); tapestry needle.

Gauge 16 sts and 24 rnds = 2" (5 cm) in St st worked in the rnd, before blocking.

LEG

With yarn doubled, CO 72 sts onto 1 needle. Divide sts evenly on 3 needles (24 sts each needle). Join for working in the rnd, being careful not to twist sts, and place marker (pm) after first st to denote beg of rnd. Cut off extra strand of yarn; cont with single strand.

Rnds 1–15: *K2, p2; rep from *—piece should measure about 1¼" (3.2 cm) from beg after completing Rnd 15.

Rnd 16: Knit

Rnds 17 and 18: Purl.

Rnd 19: Knit.

Rnds 20 and 21: *K2, p2; rep from *.

Rnds 22 and 23: *P2, k2; rep from *.

Rnds 24–31: Rep Rnds 20–23 two times.

Rnd 32: Knit.

Rnds 33 and 34: Purl.

Rnd 35: Knit.

Rnds 36–49: *K2, p2; rep from *.

Rnd 50: Knit to last 2 sts of rnd, p2tog (this becomes the "seam" st at center back leg)—71 sts rem.

Rnds 51–71: K70, p1—piece should measure about 6" (15 cm) from beg after completing Rnd 71. Beg textured patt for front of leg and instep as foll:

Rnds 72 and 73: K26, [p2, k6] 2 times, p2, k26, p1.

Rnds 74 and 75: K22, pm on Rnd 74, [k2, p2,] 6 times, k2, pm on Rnd 74, k22, p1.

Rnds 76 and 77: Knit to m, slip marker (sl m), [p2, k2] 6 times, p2, sl m, knit to last st, p1.

Rnds 78 and 79: Knit to m, sl m, [k2, p2] 6 times, k2, sl m, knit to last st, p1.

Rnds 80–109: Rep the Rnds 76–79 seven more times, then rep Rnds 76 and 77 once more, and *at the same time* dec 1 st each side of seam st on Rnds 80, 86, 92, 98, and 104 as foll: Sl 1, k1, psso, work in patts to last 3 sts, k2tog, p1—2 sts dec'd per dec rnd; 61 sts rem after all decs have been worked. When Rnd 109 has been completed, cut yarn.

HEEL

Heel flap: Place 15 sts on each side of seam st, plus the seam st itself, onto 1 needle to work for heel flap—31 sts. Hold rem 30 sts on 2 needles to be worked later for instep. With RS facing, join yarn to beg of heel sts. Work 31 heel sts back and forth in rows as foll:

Row 1: (RS) Sl 1, k4, k2tog, k5, k2tog, k1, p1 (seam st), k1, [k2tog, k5] 2 times—27 sts rem.

Hershey chocolate bar introduced in the U.S.	A.C. Doyle publishes *Adventures of Sherlock Holmes*	X-rays developed in Germany	First kiss on the silver screen	Ice cream cone invented	Lifebuoy soap launched by W. Lever Co.	Aspirin invented by F. Bayer and Co.	First hand-held electric hair dryer	Johann Vaaler patents paper clips	First driving school in England	Upright electric vacuum cleaner	Gas-powered lawn mower
1894		1895	1896		1897	1899		1900	1901		1902

Row 2: (WS) Sl 1, p12, k1, p13.

Row 3: [Sl 1, k1] 3 times, sl 1, k2tog, [sl 1, k1] 9 times—26 sts rem.

Row 4: Sl 1, purl to end.

Row 5: *Sl 1, k1; rep from *.

Rep the last 2 rows 13 more times, then work Row 4 (WS) once more—32 rows total; 16 chain sts (slipped selvedge sts) along edge of heel flap.

Turn heel: Work short rows as foll:

Row 1: (RS) Sl 1, k16, k2tog, turn.

Row 2: (WS) Sl 1, p8, p2tog, turn.

Row 3: Sl 1, k8, k2tog, turn.

Rep Rows 2 and 3 until all heel sts have been worked, ending with a WS row—10 heel sts rem.

Gussets: Rejoin for working in the rnd as foll:

Rnd 1: With needle 1, k10 heel sts, then pick up and knit 16 sts along right side of heel flap; with needle 2, k2, work instep patt (see above) over center 26 sts, k2; with needle 3, pick up and knit 16 sts along left side of heel flap, then knit the first 5 sts from needle 1 again—72 sts total; 21 sts each on needles 1 and 3, 30 instep sts on needle 2. Rnd begins at back of heel.

Rnd 2: On needle 1, knit to last 3 sts, k2tog, k1; on needle 2, work instep sts as established; on needle 3, k1, sl 1, k1, psso, knit to end—2 sts dec'd.

Rnd 3: On needle 1, knit; on needle 2, work instep sts as established; on needle 3, knit. Rep Rnds 2 and 3 seven more times—56 sts rem; 13 sts each on needles 1 and 3, 30 instep sts on needle 2.

FOOT

Cont even as established until 54 rnds have been worked from gusset pick-up rnd, ending with Rnd 2 of instep patt—foot should

---

INSTEP PATTERN (worked over 26 sts)

Rnds 1 and 2: [K2, p2] 6 times, k2.
Rnds 3 and 4: [P2, k2] 6 times, p2.
Repeat Rnds 1–4 for pattern.

---

measure 6¼" (16 cm) from back of heel, or 2¾" (7 cm) less than desired total length.

TOE

Rnds 1 and 2: Knit to marked instep sts, sl m, k4, [p2, k2] 4 times, p2, k4, sl m, knit to end of rnd.

Rnds 3 and 4: Knit to marked instep sts, sl m, k6, [p2, k2] 3 times, p2, k6, sl m, knit to end of rnd.

Rnds 5 and 6: Knit to marked instep sts, sl m, k8, [p2, k2] 2 times, p2, k8, sl m, knit to end of rnd.

Rnds 7 and 8: Knit to marked instep sts, sl m, k10, p2, k2, p2, k10, sl m, knit to end of rnd.

Rnds 9 and 10: Knit to marked instep sts, sl m, k12, p2, k12, sl m, knit to end.

Rnds 11–15: Knit.

Rnd 16: *P2 tog, k5; rep from *—48 sts rem.

Rnds 17–19: Knit.

Rnd 20: *P2tog, k4; rep from *—40 sts rem.

Rnds 21–24: Knit.

Rnd 25: *P2tog, k3; rep from *—32 sts rem.

Rnds 26–28: Knit.

Rnd 29: *P2tog, k2; rep from *—24 sts rem.

Rnds 30 and 31: Knit.

Rnd 32: *P2tog, k1; rep from *—16 sts rem.

Rnds 33 and 34: Knit.

Cut yarn, thread tail on a tapestry needle, draw through rem sts, and pull up snugly to close end of toe. Weave in loose ends. Block on sock blockers or under a damp towel.

First automatic tea maker	Thomas Sullivan invents the tea bag	Electric washing machine launched in the U.S.	Rowenta launches electric iron	Bleriot flies across the English Channel	Neon lighting invented	Coco Chanel launches women's sportswear	Wristwatch becomes popular for men	Deep-freeze invented	In Britain, men over 21 and women over 30 with property allowed to vote	Universal adult suffrage in the U.K. adds women 21 to 30 and abolishes property qualification
1902	1904	1907	1908	1909	1910	1913	1914	1917	1918	1928

INFANT'S FANCY SILK SOCK

First Size

Weldon's, *Volume 24, Seventy-fifth Series,*
1909, page 12

Original specifies 1 ounce of Maygrove's Knitting
Silk in white, cream, or pale pink; four steel #16
(U.S. 0000; 1.25 mm) needles.

This tiny sock has the look and construction of an adult sock, but in miniature. I've used a wool-blend sock yarn rather than "knitting silk" and U.S. size 00 (1.75 mm) needles instead of the size 0000 (1.25 mm) needles called for in the original pattern.

Other than that, I've made this tiny sock exactly as the pattern is written, with a Dutch Heel and Round Toe. I suspect that the original knitted sock was only slightly smaller than my interpretation.

SPECIFICATIONS

Finished Size 4½" (11.5 cm) foot circumference, 4¾" (12 cm) long from cast-on edge to top of heel flap, and 4¼" (11 cm) long from back of heel to tip of toe. To fit U.S. infants' shoe sizes about 3 to 4.

Yarn About 215 yd (196 m) of fingering-weight (Super Fine #1) yarn. **We used** Lorna's Laces Shepherd Sock (75% wool, 25% nylon; 215 yd [196 m]/2 oz; 21 wraps per inch): #0ns natural, 1 skein.

Needles Size 00 (1.75 mm): set of 4 double-pointed. Adjust needle size if necessary to obtain the correct gauge.

Notions Stitch marker (m); tapestry needle.

Gauge 10½ sts and 13 rnds = 1" (2.5 cm) in St st worked in the rnd, before blocking.

LEG PATTERN
(multiple of 4 sts)
Rnd 1: *K1, yo, k2tog, p1; rep from *.
Rnds 2 and 4: *K3, p1; rep from *.
Rnd 3: *Yo, k2tog, k1, p1; rep from *.
Rep Rnds 1–4 for pattern.

LEG

Holding 2 needles tog, CO 48 sts. Remove 1 needle from CO sts. Divide sts evenly onto 3 needles (16 sts each needle). Join for working in the rnd, being careful not to twist sts, and place marker (pm) after first st to denote beg of rnd.

Cuff: Work k2, p2 ribbing for 21 rnds— piece should measure 1½" (3.8 cm) from beg.

Leg: Rep 4 rnds of leg patt (see above) 10 times total—40 patt rnds completed; piece should measure about 4¾" (12 cm) from beg.

HEEL

Heel flap: [Sl 1, k1] 3 times, sl 1, [k2tog, sl 1] 5 times, [k1, sl 1] 2 times, k1—22 heel sts. Hold rem 21 sts on 2 needles to be worked later for instep (first and last sts on instep needle are purl sts). Work 22 heel sts back and forth in rows as foll:

Row 1: (WS) Sl 1, p21.

Row 2: (RS) *Sl 1, k1; rep from *.

Rep Rows 1 and 2 until a total of 24 rows have been worked, ending with a WS row— 12 chain sts (slipped selvedge sts) along each edge of heel flap.

Hershey chocolate bar introduced in the U.S.	A.C. Doyle publishes *Adventures of Sherlock Holmes*	X-rays developed in Germany	First kiss on the silver screen	Ice cream cone invented	Lifebuoy soap launched by W. Lever Co.	Aspirin invented by F. Bayer and Co.	First hand-held electric hair dryer	Johann Vaaler patents paper clips	First driving school in England	Upright electric vacuum cleaner	Gas-powered lawn mower
1894		1895	1896		1897	1899		1900	1901		1902

Turn heel: Cont in short rows as foll:

Row 1: (RS) Sl 1, k13, k2tog, turn.

Row 2: (WS) Sl 1, p6, p2tog, turn.

Row 3: Sl 1, k6, k2tog, turn.

Rep Rows 2 and 3 until 8 sts rem, ending with a WS row. *Next row:* Sl 1, k1, [k2tog] 2 times, k2—6 sts rem.

Gussets: Rejoin for working in the rnd as foll:

Rnd 1: With needle holding 6 heel sts (needle 1), pick up and knit 12 sts along right side of heel flap; with needle 2, p1, work Rnd 1 of leg patt over next 20 sts; with needle 3, pick up and knit 12 sts along left side of heel flap, then knit the first 3 sts from needle 1 again—51 sts total; 15 sts each on needles 1 and 3, 21 instep sts on needle 2. Rnd begins at back of heel.

Rnd 2: On needle 1, knit to last 3 sts, k2tog, k1; on needle 2, p1, work 20 sts in leg patt as established; on needle 3, k1, sl 1, k1, psso, knit to end—2 sts dec'd.

Rnd 3: On needle 1, knit; on needle 2, work instep sts as established; on needle 3, knit.

Rep Rnds 2 and 3 two more times—45 sts rem; 12 sts each on needles 1 and 3, 21 instep sts on needle 2.

FOOT

Cont as established, working the heel sts in St st and the instep sts in patt until foot measures 3¼" (8.5 cm), or 1" (2.5 cm) less than desired total length.

TOE

Rnd 1: *K2tog, k3; rep from *—36 sts rem.

Rnds 2–4: Knit.

Rnd 5: *K2tog, k2; rep from *—27 sts rem.

Rnds 6 and 7: Knit even.

Rnd 8: *K2tog, k1; rep from *—18 sts rem.

Rnds 9 and 10: Knit even.

Rnd 11: *K2tog; rep from *—9 sts rem.

Cut yarn, thread tail on a tapestry needle, draw tail through rem sts, and pull up snugly to close end of toe. Weave in loose ends. Block on sock blockers or under a damp towel.

First automatic tea maker	Thomas Sullivan invents the tea bag	Electric washing machine launched in the U.S.	Rowenta launches electric iron	Bleriot flies across the English Channel	Neon lighting invented	Coco Chanel launches women's sportswear	Wristwatch becomes popular for men	Deep-freeze invented	In Britain, men over 21 and women over 30 with property allowed to vote	Universal adult suffrage in the U.K. adds women 21 to 30 and abolishes property qualification
1902	1904	1907	1908	1909	1910	1913	1914	1917	1918	1928

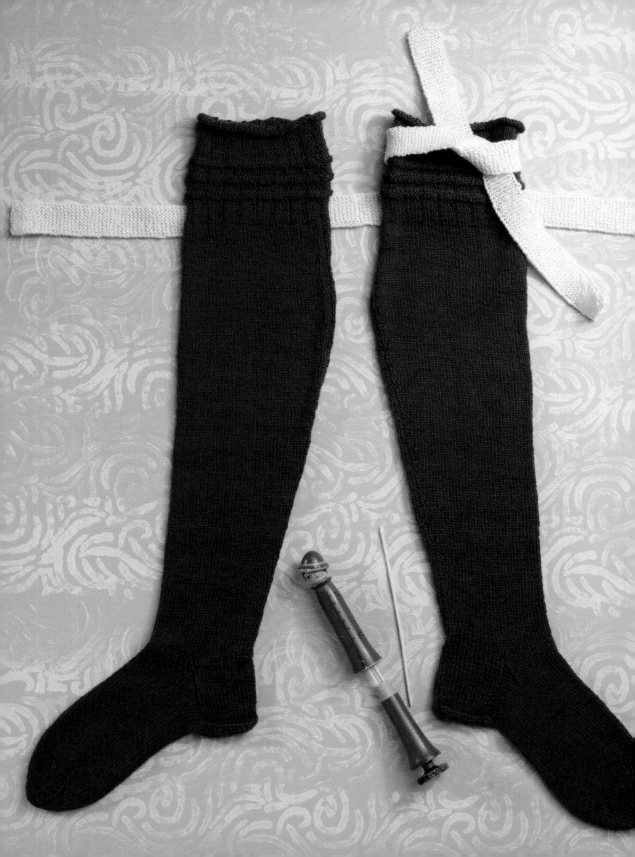

LADIES USEFUL STOCKINGS

Weldon's, Volume 28, Eighty-ninth Series, 1913, page 14

Original specifies 5 ounces of Patons Rose Fingering Wool; four steel #13 (U.S. 0; 2 mm) needles.

I feel that this stocking—for that is truly what it is, long and shaped—suits those who do reenactments or belong to the Society for Creative Anachronism, if no one else. I've kept to the pattern for the most part, working a Dutch Heel and Flat Toe, but I've adjusted the order in which the stitches are decreased for the gussets, so that the round begins at the back of the heel.

In the past, knitted garters would have held up this type of stocking. These garters were narrow strips of knitting, about 30" (76 cm) long and 2¼" (5.5 cm) wide. According to *The Workwoman's Guide*, garters were typically made of "worsted, cotton, or soft wool" worked on 12 to 30 stitches, depending on the thickness of the yarn. They were most commonly worked in garter stitch (knit every row), but ribbing, stockinette stitch, or "a succession of squares of different patterns" were also used.

SPECIFICATIONS

Finished Size Stockings: 7" (18 cm) foot circumference, 22" (56 cm) long from cast-on edge to top of heel flap, and 9½" (24 cm) long from back of heel to tip of toe. To fit women's U.S. shoe sizes 8 to 9. Garters: 1¼" (3.2 cm) wide and 28" (71 cm) long.

Yarn About 740 yd (677 m) of fingering-weight (Super Fine #1) yarn for stockings; about 95 yd (87 m) of Fine #1 yarn for garters. **We used** for the stockings: Gems Pearl (100% merino; 185 yd [170 m]/50 g; 21 wraps per inch): #57 French blue, 4 skeins. (*Note:* You'll need 5 skeins if you lengthen the leg or foot.) For the garters: About 1 oz (28 g) of fingering-weight yarn in natural.

Needles Size 1 (2.5 mm): set of 4 double-pointed. Adjust needle size if necessary to obtain the correct gauge.

Notions Stitch marker (m); tapestry needle.

Gauge 16 sts and 20 rnds = 2" (5 cm) in St st using stocking yarn and worked in the rnd, before blocking.

LEG

With main yarn doubled, CO 90 sts onto 1 needle. Divide sts evenly onto 3 needles (30 sts each needle). Join for working in the rnd, being careful not to twist sts, and place marker (pm) after first st to denote beg of rnd. Cut off second strand of yarn; work to end with single strand. Knit 1 rnd.

Cuff: *K4, p1; rep from * to end of rnd. Rep this rnd 20 more times—21 rnds total; piece measures about 2" (5 cm) from beg.

Leg: Work patt as foll:

Rnd 1: Knit.

Rnds 2–4: Purl.

Rnd 5: Knit.

Rnds 6–9: *K4, p1; rep from *.

Rnds 10–27: Rep Rnds 1–9 two more times.

Rnds 28–33: Rep Rnd 6 six times.

On the next rnd, knit to last st, end p1 ("seam" st). Rep the last rnd until piece measures 6" (15 cm) from CO. *Inc rnd:* K1, M1 (Glossary, page 115), knit to last 2 sts, M1, k1, p1—2 sts inc'd. Work 4 rnds even (knit to last st, end p1). Rep the last 5 rnds once, then work inc rnd once more—96 sts. Work 7 rnds even—piece should measure about 7¾" (19.5 cm) from CO. *Dec rnd:* K1, sl 1, k1, psso, knit to last 4 sts, k2tog, k1, p1—2 sts dec'd. Work 7 rnds even. Rep the last 8 rnds 18 more times—58 sts; piece should measure about 22" (56 cm) from beg. *Next rnd:* Knit to last16 sts of the rnd.

HEEL

Heel flap: Place the next 31 sts (unworked 16 sts from end of previous rnd and first 15 sts of next rnd) onto one needle to work for heel; the purled seam st from the back of the leg should be in the center of the heel needle. Hold rem 27 sts on 2 needles to be worked later for instep. Work 31 heel sts back and forth in rows as foll:

Row 1: (RS) Sl 1, k30.

Row 2: (WS) Sl 1, p30.

Rep Rows 1 and 2 until a total of 30 rows have been worked, ending with a WS row—15 chain sts (slipped selvedge sts) along each edge of heel flap.

Turn heel: Work short rows as foll:

Row 1: (RS) Sl 1, k16, k2tog, turn.

Row 2: (WS) Sl 1, p3, p2tog, turn.

Row 3: Sl 1, k3, k2tog, turn.

Row 4: Sl 1, p3, p2tog, turn.

Rep Rows 3 and 4 until all heel sts have been worked—5 heel sts rem.

Gussets: Rejoin for working in the rnd as foll:

Rnd 1: With needle 1, k5 heel sts, then pick up and knit 15 sts along right side of heel flap; with needle 2, k27 instep sts; with needle 3, pick up and knit 15 sts along left side of heel flap, then knit the first 3 sts from needle 1 again—62 sts total; 17 heel sts on needle 1, 27 instep sts on needle 2, 18 heel sts on needle 3. Rnd begins at back of heel.

Rnd 2: Knit.

Rnd 3: On needle 1, knit to last 3 sts, k2tog, k1; on needle 2, k27 instep sts; on needle 3, k1, sl 1, k1, psso, knit to end— 2 sts dec'd.

Rep Rnds 2 and 3 three more times—54 sts rem; 13 sts on needle 1, 27 instep sts on needle 2, 14 sts on needle 3.

Hershey chocolate bar introduced in the U.S.	A.C. Doyle publishes *Adventures of Sherlock Holmes*	X-rays developed in Germany	First kiss on the silver screen	Ice cream cone invented	Lifebuoy soap launched by W. Lever Co.	Aspirin invented by F. Bayer and Co.	First hand-held electric hair dryer	Johann Vaaler patents paper clips	First driving school in England	Upright electric vacuum cleaner	Gas-powered lawn mower
1894		1895	1896		1897	1899		1900	1901		1902

FOOT

Work even in St st until foot measures 7"
(18 cm) from back of heel, or 2½" (6.5 cm)
less than desired total length.

TOE

Rnd 1: On needle 1, knit to last 3 sts, k2tog,
 k1; on needle 2, k1, sl 1, k1, psso, knit to
 last 3 sts, k2tog, k1; on needle 3, k1, sl 1,
 k1, psso, knit to end—4 sts dec'd.
Rnd 2: Knit.
Rep Rnds 1 and 2 ten more times—10 sts
rem. Cut yarn, leaving a 12" (30.5-cm) tail.
Thread tail on a tapestry needle, draw
through rem sts, and pull up snugly to close
end of toe. Weave in loose ends. Block on
sock blockers or under a damp towel.

GARTERS *(make 2)*

With yarn for garters, CO 10 sts. Work
garter st (knit every row) until piece measures 28" (71 cm) from beg. BO all sts. Weave
in loose ends.

First automatic tea maker	Thomas Sullivan invents the tea bag	Electric washing machine launched in the U.S.	Rowenta launches electric iron	Bleriot flies across the English Channel	Neon lighting invented	Coco Chanel launches women's sportswear	Wristwatch becomes popular for men	Deep-freeze invented	In Britain, men over 21 and women over 30 with property allowed to vote	Universal adult suffrage in the U.K. adds women 21 to 30 and abolishes property qualification
1902	1904	1907	1908	1909	1910	1913	1914	1917	1918	1928

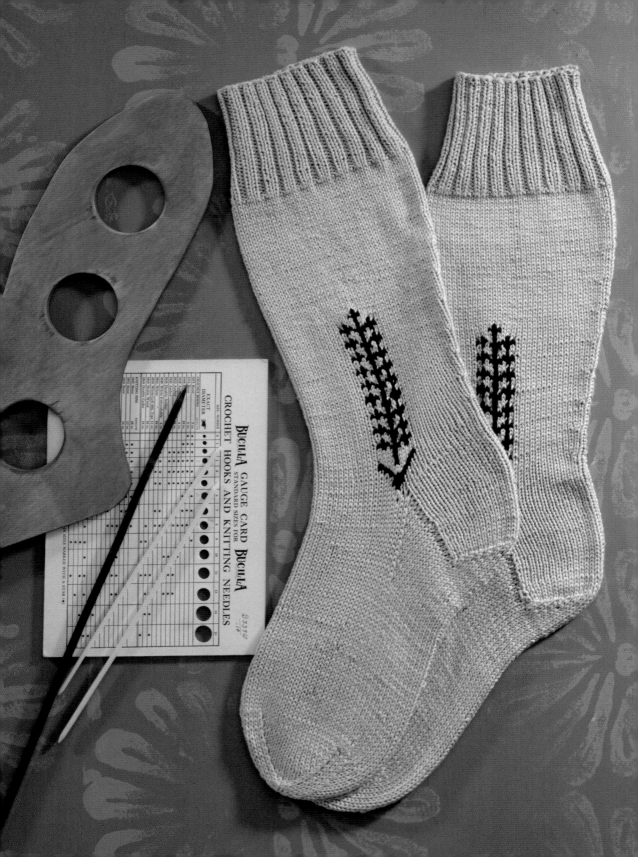

LADIES SILK STOCKINGS

with Clocks

Weldon's, *Inspired by Volume 29, Ninety-fourth Series,*
1914, page 4

Original specifies 5 ounces of Patons Rose
Fingering Wool; four steel #13 (U.S. 0; 2 mm)
needles.

The original instructions call for a true stocking with a 24" (61 cm) leg. My version is similarly elegant in design, but the shortened length is more suitable for the twenty-first century. I've used the clock patterns from Volume 8, Twenty-second Series, of *Weldon's Practical Knitter*, an entire issue dedicated to knitting numerals, letters, small figures, and clocks (originally spelled "clox") into stockings. I have followed the suggestion for 5" (12.5 cm) long clocks and have worked them as recommended, using a length of the contrasting color for the clocks stitches on one round, and bringing the contrast yarn across the back of the clocks section (leaving short floats) into position to work the clocks stitches on the next round. This stocking has a French Heel and ends in a French Toe.

SPECIFICATIONS

Finished Size 8" (20.5 cm) foot circumference, 10¼" (26 cm) long from cast-on edge to top of heel flap, and 9½" (24 cm) long from back of heel to tip of toe. To fit women's U.S. shoe sizes 8 to 9.

Yarn About 406 yd (371 m) of 1 main color and 203 yd (186 m) of 1 contrasting color of fingering-weight (Super Fine #1) yarn. **We used** Jaeger Silk 4 Ply (100% silk; 203 yd [186 m]/ 50 g; 25 wraps per inch): #131 silver blue (gray, MC), 2 skeins; #137 jet (black, CC), 1 skein. *Note:* You'll need 3 skeins MC if you lengthen the leg or foot.

Needles Size 0 (2 mm): set of 4 double-pointed. Adjust needle size if necessary to obtain the correct gauge.

Notions Stitch marker (m); removable stitch marker or safety pin; tapestry needle.

Gauge 16½ sts and 24 rnds = 2" (5 cm) in St st worked in the rnd, before blocking.

Note

The leg shaping happens at the same time as the clock pattern; please read the directions all the way through before proceeding.

LEG

With MC, CO 80 sts onto 1 needle. Divide sts as evenly as possible on 3 needles. Join for working in the rnd, being careful not to twist sts, and place marker (pm) after first st to denote beg of rnd.

Cuff: Work k2, p2 ribbing for 32 rnds—piece should measure 3" (7.5 cm) from beg.

Clock

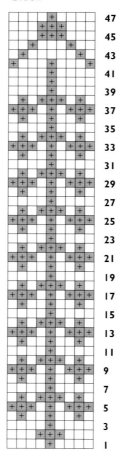

☐ gray MC

⊞ black CC

47
45
43
41
39
37
35
33
31
29
27
25
23
21
19
17
15
13
11
9
7
5
3
1

Leg: Work St st for 1½" (3.8 cm). *Dec rnd:* K1, sl 1, k1, psso, knit to last 3 sts, k2tog, k1—2 sts dec'd. Knit 7 rnds even, then rep dec rnd. Rep last 8 rnds once more—74 sts; piece measures about 6" (15 cm) from beg. Rearrange sts, if necessary, so there are 21 sts each on needles 1 and 3, and 32 instep sts on needle 2. The first and last sts of the instep needle will be the center sts of the clock motifs. Measure out 2 strands of CC about 7½ feet (2.25 m) long. On the next rnd, establish position of patts from Clock chart (at left) as foll: K17, *pm, work Rnd 1 of clock patt over next 9 sts, pm,* k22; rep from * to * once more, k17—two 9-st clock patt sections. On the foll patt rnds, carry the CC loosely across the back side of the work to avoid puckering, and bring it into position to work each rnd; twist the yarns around each other at the color changes to avoid leaving holes. Work Rnds 2–47 of Clock chart, knitting rem sts with MC, and *at the same time* dec 1 st at each end of rnd as for dec rnd on chart Rnds 8, 16, 24, 32, and 40—64 sts after Rnd 40 has been completed. When Rnd 47 of chart has been completed, cut off CC. Knit 2 rnds—piece should measure about 10¼" (26 cm) from beg.

HEEL

Heel flap: Sl 1, k15, turn work. Sl 1, p31—32 heel sts on 1 needle. Hold rem 32 sts on 2 needles to be worked later for instep. Work 32 heel sts back and forth in rows as foll:
Row 1: (RS) Sl 1, k31.
Row 2: (WS) Sl 1, p31.
Rep Rows 1 and 2 until a total of 32 rows have been worked, ending with a WS row—16 chain sts (slipped selvedge sts) along each edge of heel flap.

Hershey chocolate bar introduced in the U.S.	A.C. Doyle publishes *Adventures of Sherlock Holmes*	X-rays developed in Germany	First kiss on the silver screen	Ice cream cone invented	Lifebuoy soap launched by W. Lever Co.	Aspirin invented by F. Bayer and Co.	First hand-held electric hair dryer	Johann Vaaler patents paper clips	First driving school in England	Upright electric vacuum cleaner	Gas-powered lawn mower
1894		1895	1896		1897	1899		1900	1901		1902

Turn heel: Work short rows as foll:

Row 1: K18, sl 1, k1, psso, k1, turn.

Row 2: (WS) Sl 1, p5, p2tog, p1, turn.

Row 3: Sl 1, knit to 1 st before gap formed by previous row, sl 1, k1, psso, k1, turn.

Row 4: Sl 1, purl to 1 st before gap formed by previous row, p2tog, p1, turn.

Rep Rows 3 and 4 until all heel sts have been worked—18 heel sts rem.

Gussets: Rejoin for working in the rnd as foll:

Rnd 1: With needle 1, k18 heel sts, then pick up and knit 16 sts along right side of heel flap; with needle 2, k32 instep sts; with needle 3, pick up and knit 16 sts along left side of heel flap, then knit the first 9 sts from needle 1 again—82 sts total; 25 sts each on needles 1 and 3, 32 instep sts on needle 2. Rnd begins at back of heel.

Rnd 2: On needle 1, knit to last 3 sts, k2tog, k1; on needle 2, k32 instep sts; on needle 3, k1, sl 1, k1, psso, knit to end—2 sts dec'd.

Rnd 3: Knit.

Rep Rnds 2 and 3 seven more times—66 sts rem; 17 sts each on needles 1 and 3, 32 instep sts on needle 2.

FOOT

Cont even in St st until foot measures 8" (20.5 cm) from back of heel, or 1½" (3.8 cm) less than desired total length, ending last rnd 11 sts from the end of needle 3.

TOE

Rearrange sts so that there are 22 sts each on 3 needles as foll: Last 11 unworked sts of previous rnd and first 11 sts of rnd on one needle (new needle 1); rem 6 sts from old needle 1 and first 16 instep sts on one needle (new needle 2); rem 16 sts of old instep needle and first 6 sts of old needle 3 on one needle (new needle 3)—center of instep sts is now between new needles 2 and 3.

Rnd 1: *Kl, sl 1, k1, psso, work to last 3 sts on needle, k2tog, k1; rep from * 2 more times—6 sts dec'd.

Rnd 2: Knit.

Rep Rnds 1 and 2 eight more times—12 sts rem. Cut yarn, leaving a 12" (30.5-cm) tail. Thread tail on a tapestry needle, draw through rem sts, and pull up snugly to close end of toe. Weave in loose ends. Block on sock blockers or under a damp towel.

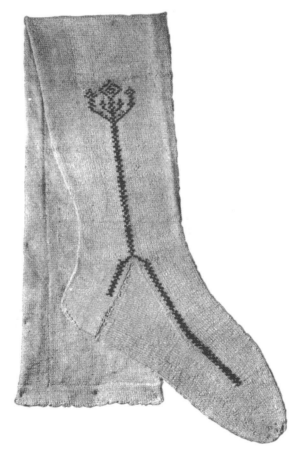

First automatic tea maker	Thomas Sullivan invents the tea bag	Electric washing machine launched in the U.S.	Rowenta launches electric iron	Bleriot flies across the English Channel	Neon lighting invented	Coco Chanel launches women's sportswear	Wristwatch becomes popular for men	Deep-freeze invented	In Britain, men over 21 and women over 30 with property allowed to vote	Universal adult suffrage in the U.K. adds women 21 to 30 and abolishes property qualification
1902	1904	1907	1908	1909	1910	1913	1914	1917	1918	1928

ABBREVIATIONS

beg	begin(s); beginning
BO	bind off
CC	contrasting color
cm	centimeter(s)
cn	cable needle
CO	cast on
cont	continue(s); continuing
dec	decrease(s); decreasing
dpn	double-pointed needle(s)
est	established
even	work without increasing or decreasing
foll	follow(s); following
g	gram(s)
inc	increase(s); increasing
k	knit
k2tog	knit 2 stitches together
kwise	knitwise
m	marker(s)
MC	main color
mm	millimeter(s)
p	purl
patt	pattern(s)
pm	place marker(s)
psso	pass slipped stitch over
p2tog	purl 2 stitches together
pwise	purlwise
rem	remain(s); remaining
rep	repeat(s); repeating
rev	reverse
rnd(s)	round(s)
RS	right side
sl	slip
st(s)	stitch(es)
St st	stockinette stitch
tog	together
WS	wrong side
yo	yarn over

GLOSSARY

CAST-ONS

Continental/Long-Tail Cast-On

Place a slipknot on the right-hand needle, leaving a long tail (about an inch in length for every stitch to be cast-on is a safe estimate). Place the thumb and index finger of your left hand between the two strands of yarn. Secure the long ends by closing your other three fingers on them. Twist your wrist so that your palm points upwards, and spread your thumb and index finger apart to make a V of the yarn around them (Figure 1). *Place the needle in front of the yarn around your thumb and bring it upward through the loop (Figure 2). Place the needle over the top of the yarn around your index finger and bring the needle down through the loop around your thumb (Figure 3). Drop the loop off your thumb and, placing your thumb back in the V formation, tighten up the resulting stitch on the needle (Figure 4). Repeat from * until the desired number of stitches have been cast on.

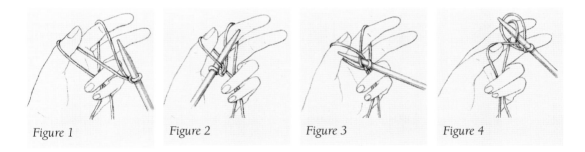

Figure 1   Figure 2   Figure 3   Figure 4

Knitted Cast-On

Place a slipknot on the left-hand needle. The slipknot counts as the first stitch. *With right-hand needle, knit into the first loop on left needle (Figure 1) and place new loop onto the left needle (Figure 2)—2 stitches on left needle. Repeat from *, always working into the last stitch made.

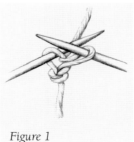

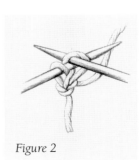

Figure 1   Figure 2

DECREASES

Knit 2 Together (k2tog) Decrease

Knit 2 stitches together as if they were a single stitch.

k2tog

Slip 1, Knit 1, Pass Slipped Stitch Over (sl 1, k1, psso) Decrease

Slip 1 stitch onto right needle knit-wise, knit the next stitch (Figure 1), then use the left needle tip to pick the slipped stitch over the knitted stitch and drop this stitch off the nee-dle (Figure 2).

Figure 1

Figure 2

Slip, Slip, Knit (ssk) Decrease

This decrease gives the same result as "sl 1, k1, psso," but was not in general use when *Weldon's* was written, or at least there's no evidence that it was. You may replace the "sl 1, k1, psso" decrease, with this method.

Slip 2 stitches, one at a time, knit-wise, to the right needle (Figure 1). Insert the tip of the left needle into the front of these two stitches and knit them together through their back loops with the right needle (Figure 2).

Figure 1

Figure 2

Purl 2 Together (p2tog) Decrease

Purl 2 stitches together as if they were as single stitch.

p2tog

INCREASES

Make 1 (M1) Increase
Use the right needle tip to pick up the bar between the stitch you just worked and the next one to be worked, place it on the left-hand needle (Figure 1), then knit into the back of this picked-up stitch (Figure 2). This tightens the stitch up and makes an almost invisible stitch.

Figure 1

Figure 2

Make 1 Purlwise (M1 pwise) Increase
Use the left needle tip to pick up the bar from back to front between the stitch you just worked and the next one to be worked (Figure 1), and purl into the front of this picked-up stitch (Figure 2).

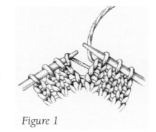

Figure 1

Figure 2

JOIN NEW YARN

Splice Method
This is a tidy method to join a new ball of yarn, but it only works with pure wool or wool blended with another animal fiber (such as mohair). This method will not work with washable wool, synthetic fibers, cotton, or silk.

Untwist an inch or two of both the old and new yarn (Figure 1). Overlap the unraveled ends (Figure 2), and moisten them (you may use water, but saliva works best). Place this wet section of overlapping yarn between the palms of your two hands and quickly roll your hands back and forth (Figure 3) to make the fibers stick and hold together (essentially felting them). The join will hold firm enough to continue knitting right away—you needn't wait for the yarn to dry.

Figure 1

Figure 2

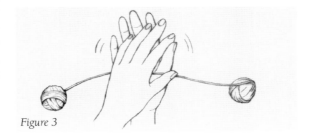

Figure 3

JOIN STITCHES INTO A ROUND

Cross-Over Join

Slip the first cast-on stitch (it will be at the left needle tip) onto the right needle (Figure 1). With the left needle, pick up the last cast-on stitch (now the second stitch on the right needle), bring it up over the top of the previously moved stitch (Figure 2), and place it on the tip of the left needle (Figure 3). In essence, the first and last stitches have changed places, and the last stitch cast-on will surround the first.

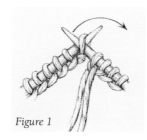

Figure 1

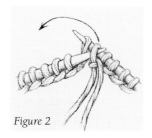

Figure 2

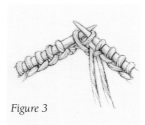

Figure 3

Extra Stitch Join

This method involves casting on one more stitch than intended. Slip this extra stitch onto the left needle, next to the first stitch cast-on (Figure 4), and knit these two stitches together (Figure 5), thereby joining the first and last stitches and decreasing to the correct number of stitches.

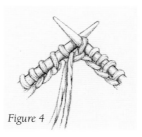

Figure 4

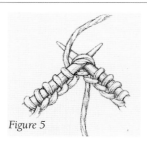

Figure 5

Two-End Join

Work the first two or three stitches of the round with both ends of yarn used for casting on (Figure 6). In other words, use the yarn attached to the ball and the tail that remains from casting on to work these stitches. After you have joined and worked several stitches, drop the tail end and continue with the yarn attached to the ball. Remember that the join stitches are doubled on the next round; work them as single stitches.

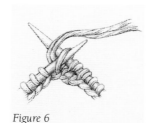

Figure 6

TOE FINISHES

Kitchener Stitch

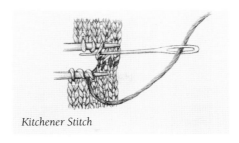

Place the stitches to be joined on two separate knitting needles held parallel with the tips pointing to the right. Cut the working yarn, leaving a tail about 12" (30.5 cm) long, and thread this tail on a tapestry needle. Work the threaded needle back and forth between the stitches on the two knitting needles as follows:

Step 1: Bring the threaded needle through the first stitch on the front needle as if to purl and leave this stitch on the needle.

Step 2: Bring the threaded needle through the first stitch on the back needle as if to knit and leave this stitch on the needle.

Step 3: Bring the threaded needle through the first stitch on the front needle (the same stitch used previously) as if to knit and slip this stitch off the needle. Bring the threaded needle through the next st on the front needle (now the first

Kitchener Stitch

stitch) as if to purl and leave this stitch on the needle.

Step 4: Bring the threaded needle through the first stitch on the back needle (the same stitch used previously) as if to purl (illustrated) and slip this stitch off the needle. Bring the threaded needle through the next stitch on the back needle (now the first stitch) as if to knit and leave this stitch on the needle.

Repeat Steps 3 and 4 until no stitches remain on the needles.

Gathered Tip

Cut the working yarn, leaving a tail about 8" (20.5 cm) long. Thread the tail on a tapestry needle, run the needle through each live stitch, removing the stitch from the knitting needle as you do so (Figure 1), then pull to tighten and close the opening (Figure 2). Weave in the yarn end on the inside of the piece and secure.

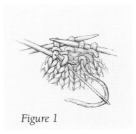

Figure 1

Figure 2

WRAPS PER INCH

Wraps per inch (wpi) is the number of strands of yarn that can fit side by side in a distance of one inch. It is a useful way to determine if a different (or hand-spun) yarn can be substituted for the yarn used in the project. Compare the weight of your yarn to the project yarn by comparing wraps per inch (listed with the yarn specifications for each project). Wrap your yarn around a ruler for one inch and count the number of wraps. If you have more wraps per inch than specified in the pattern, your yarn is too thin; fewer wraps per inch, your yarn is too thick.

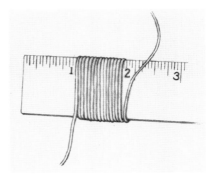

BIBLIOGRAPHY

A Lady. *The Workwoman's Guide*, facsimile reproduction of the 1938 edition. Guilford, Connecticut: Opus Publications.

Harvey, Michael. *Patons, a Story of Handknitting*. Ascot, United Kingdom: Springwood Books, 1985.

Rutt, Richard. *A History of Hand Knitting*. London: B.T. Batsford, 1987 (republished by Interweave Press in 2003).

NOTE: *Weldon's Practical Needlework*, Volumes 1 through 12, are available for $30 each from Interweave Press LLC, 201 East Fourth St., Loveland, CO 80537; (800) 272-2193; www.interweave.com.

Weldon's Practical Needlework, Vol. 1–30, 1886–1915.

Williams, Neville. *Chronology of World History 1776–1900*, Vol. III. Santa Barbara, California: ABC Clio.

——.*1901–1998, The Modern World*.

Yarn Suppliers
A special thanks to the companies listed below who donated yarn for the projects in this book.

The Alpaca Yarn Company
(formerly the Yarn Division of the AFCNA/America's Alpaca)
144 Roosevelt Ave. Bay #1
York, PA 17404
(866) 440-7222
www.thealpacayarnco.com
Glimmer

Berroco
PO Box 367
Uxbridge, MA 01569
(508) 278-2527
www.berroco.com
Sunbeam St. Ives

Dale of Norway
N16 W23390 Stoneridge Dr.,
Ste. A
Waukesha, WI 53188
(262) 544-1996
www.dale.no
Baby Ull

Lorna's Laces
4229 N. Honore St.
Chicago, IL 60613
(773) 935-3803
www.lornaslaces.net
Shepherd Sock Yarn

Louet Sales
RR 4
Prescott, ON,
Canada K0E 1T0
or
808 Commerce Park Dr.
Odgensburg, NY 13669
www.louet.com
Gems Pearl

Mountain Colors
PO Box 156
Corvallis, MT 59828
(406) 961-1900
www.mountaincolors.com
Cashmere
Weavers Wool Quarters

Russi Sales
605 Clark Rd.
Bellingham, WA 98225
(800) 950-1078
www.russisales.com
Heirloom Argyle

Schaefer Yarn Company
3514 Kelly's Corners Rd.
Interlaken, NY 14847
(607) 532-9452
www.schaeferyarn.com
Anne

Skacel Inc.
PO Box 88110
Seattle, WA 98138
www.skacelknitting.com
Fortissima/Socka

Westminster Fibers
5 Northern Blvd., Ste. 3
Amherst, NH 03031
www.knitrowan.com
Jaeger Silk 4 Ply
Jaeger Matchmaker Merino
4 Ply

The Wooly West
PO Box 58306
Salt Lake City, UT 84158
(801) 581-9812
www.woolywest.com
Footpath

INDEX